AS YOU WERE

AS
YOU
WERE

— A MEMOIR —

DAVID TROMBLAY

DZANC
BOOKS

DZANC BOOKS

5220 Dexter Ann Arbor Rd.
Ann Arbor, MI 48103
www.dzancbooks.org

First Edition: February 2021
Cover design by Matthew Revert
Interior design by Michelle Dotter

Printed in the United States of America

10   9   8   7   6   5   4   3   2   1

You shall know the truth and the truth shall make you odd.

— Flannery O'Connor, allegedly

OFF THE RESERVATION

YOU COULD BEGIN THIS WITH how Grandpa Bullshit was an arm breaker for the Irish mob in Chicago. Or how the spring of '68 became the boiling point for the Civil Rights Movement after Dr. Martin Luther King Junior's murder, shortly after Mom turned eleven. Or how she and all her siblings attended elementary school with the Jackson Five in Gary, Indiana, before they went to Hollywood and the Lynns made their way to the woods in the middle-of-nowhere Minnesota. But it would take too long to give all those details and bring the story back on track. It would be a lot simpler to say how Grandpa Bullshit decided to drive his family here in sixty-eight and did so without making a single pit stop. Instead, he crammed one of those little Porta Potties families take on camping trips into the back of his '59 Cadillac hearse, along with a couple of suitcases and all six kids.

Six years later, Mom grew tired of babysitting her little brothers and sisters, so she got knocked up and married to get out of the house. Little did she know she'd have to get notes from her husband to excuse her from school once the morning sickness started, despite his being in the same grade. So she dropped out of high school and got her GED because she'll be Goddamned.

She got divorced from him before she was old enough to register to vote. Three years after she had your big brother Sam, she has you. She takes a taxicab off the Fond du Lac Indian Reservation twenty-odd miles to St. Luke's Hospital in the east end of downtown Duluth.

You'll notice there's no mention of Dad bringing Mom to the hospital, pacing the hallway outside the delivery room while waiting to hear the news, the proclamation of it, you, being a boy. He is elsewhere—with a prostitute. You'll have to pause here, collect yourself, choke back the laughter. All you can really do is laugh. Not a ha-ha laugh, but a Jesus-jumped-up-Christ-what-could-come-next? kind of laugh—or bite your cheek, or stall, one way or another, before admitting that last bit of information.

Dad doing that might make sense if you were born after midnight on a Saturday, but you were born at about a quarter to four on a Monday afternoon. The real question is: how long should someone go on thinking that's the worst thing he did that day? Because he made Mom take care of the hooker's cat while the hooker served a ninety-day jail sentence. He wasn't charged with a crime. They let him go, according to your mother. According to *his* mother, he could high dive into a manure pile and come out smelling like roses. He doesn't go completely unpunished, however; his only begotten son will not bear his last name.

Perhaps hooker isn't the right word for the woman who kept his company the afternoon you came into the world. She didn't walk the streets or work a corner. Though the apartments above the Lake View Store—the world's first indoor mall—where she calls home, do double as a brothel of sorts. Curiously enough, the National Register of Historic Places isn't in the habit of adorning dilapidated shitholes with copper plaques. And to play devil's advocate: should it be so surprising to learn the building erected to fill every need of everyone working at the steel mill in Morgan Park, Duluth, Minnesota, did, in fact, sell everything?

Morgan Park came to be for the same reason as Hershey, Pennsylvania, except there are no chocolatiers. When it first opened to the public, the Lake View Store housed a bank, a barbershop and beauty salon, a dentist's office, a grocery market, as well as a shoe store. And if it hosts the world's oldest profession now, it certainly did a century ago.

That aside, you're not special. You're not the only child to come out of Mom's second marriage. She had twins—not identical twins, but twins nevertheless. You were a dizygotic twin, meaning each fetus had a separate placenta and a separate amniotic sac. But you grow up thinking you're their only child. That's because your brother is stillborn, as was your uncle's twin, as was your great-uncle's twin—all on Mom's side, of course.

Maybe it's genetic, or happenstance, or the scientific hypothetical sum and substance of someone hanging around a bar, begging her husband to come home, striking up a conversation with the bartender when her husband refuses to move a muscle, and eventually marrying said bartender. The above is an abridged version of how this happens. How *you* happen. It's also from whence the butterfly that peeks out from behind her bra strap came. She got her first and only tattoo one night at a bar while pregnant with the two of you.

There once was an artist who always carried a tackle box filled with tattoo guns and inks and needles, and who was more than willing to tattoo a tit for free on ladies' night. This, too, explains why your skin is stained with every color of the rainbow—how tattoos got into your blood before birth—like a crack baby, only the addiction is ink. Mom drank and smoked a bit while pregnant, too. It's easy enough to imagine her Marlboro Reds and the ladies' night drink specials played into the loss of your brother's life. At least, they do in the version she told. But in her defense, the doctors didn't know it was bad for babies back then—or so she said.

You bring up Mom's drinking and smoking while pregnant—with Bible in hand—and point out a passage, the story of when the Virgin learns she will conceive and give birth to a son. "The angel warns her away from wine and strong drink," you say. But Mom reminds you, "You're a son of a bitch, not the Son of God," and pushes you out of her way with the tip of a wooden spoon, goes back to making dinner, smirking, smiling, laughing at her own joke.

The reason for your twin brother's birth defect(s) is that all the toxins Mom put into her body went to him first. It sounds bullshitty, but it's in keeping with the summation the doctor gives after he finishes your football physical and asks if you have any questions. You seize the opportunity to ask what happened to your twin brother.

Mom doesn't know what they did with him after they took him away. He was medical waste, as far as she knows. Like the placenta and afterbirth. But the doctor should know. He delivered you and cared for you right up until you left for boot camp.

You weren't born at the Catholic hospital, which has a special plot for all the stillborns and preemies who never get to go home. You were born at the other hospital, so your twin will always be a nameless, missing thing.

Dad never says word one about a twin. When Mom does, it comes out in casual conversation. She assumed someone told you in the decade you lived with Grandma Audrey. The truth of it, and the way Mom tells you, devastates her more than it does you. Learning you shared a womb with a dead kid gives you a lifetime of things to ponder. As does her referring to you as her number two son, wondering whether she merely means you are her second-oldest living son, or if it's like in the movie *Twins*, and you're Danny DeVito in this scenario—the leftover shit.

When your brother came into this world, ruddy yet lifeless, neither she nor the doctor knew you were waiting in the wings. Two weeks after she delivered him, she went back in for a routine checkup to make sure she was still in good health, infection-free, and what have you.

That's when she found out about you.

She is alone when she learns this. Dad only knows his only son died. He's out fucking anything he can—even if he has to pay—if only to spread his seed and prove he's man enough to make a son. This is your SWAG, of course—your Scientific Wild-Ass Guess—but knowing him, and with what's known about his TBI and the historical happenings of his alcoholic-driven logic, it makes the most sense.

The way Mom tells it, you were a tiny thing tucked up under the right side of her ribcage. She explains how the doctor let her carry you around a little longer. A week or so later, they tried to induce her—but you would not budge. She chuckles when she tells that part of the story, calls you a stubborn little bastard. Shortly thereafter, the sonogram showed you were a sickly child, one losing weight with a heartbeat nowhere near as strong as the doctor preferred. A Cesarean section got scheduled, but you came to town kicking and screaming three days prior.

The cab driver took more than an hour to pick up Mom, but she didn't give them a call until after she gave up trying to track down Dad. She had her driver's license, yes, but he took the Duster days before. She took her driver's test when she was six months along with the two of you. "The guy in the passenger seat thought I'd pop at any minute," she says. "He looked like he was shitting nickels the whole time, so we were back in the DMV parking lot in less than five minutes. He didn't mark off a single mistake I made, afraid to give me any anxiety and send me into labor. I had to have the seat so far back I could barely touch the pedals," she says, and scoots back on the kitchen stool, kicking her legs like Shirley Temple.

Once she checked into the hospital, got placed on a gurney, met with her doctor, and got sent down the hallway toward the delivery room, she finally allowed herself to relax enough to let you into this world.

Your first glimpse of the St. Luke's Hospital came while she was still on her way to the delivery room but within sight of the double doors. You know, kind of like when you eat some bad Mexican food, and you're searching for a bathroom, and when you finally catch a glimpse of the porcelain bowl your sphincter lets loose a few feet shy of sitting down.

Mom learned the particulars concerning Dad's whereabouts while she was still in the hospital but takes her anger out on you. Sweet, less-than-one-week-old, nameless you.

Mom did not christen you with her married name. Instead, she gave you her maiden name: Lynn. Completely understandable. But what gives you trouble in the search for forgiveness is the business of her naming you after the most famous and accomplished man in American history. A newspaperman, inventor, musician, statesman, postmaster, ambassador, and the only non-president to have his likeness etched onto the currency, and the highest denomination at that. Yes, she named you Benjamin Frank Lynn—until Grandma Audrey intervened.

There must be a direct correlation between the absurdity of one's given name and the age of the parents at the time of their birth. Take those twins from high school, for instance. Phyllis and her brother Phallus. Their mother was seventeen when they were born. He pronounces his name *Fay-less*, like the shoe store, except with an F. And who could blame him?

But considering who you were named after, you take it upon yourself to inform him his parents named him for a dildo. He can't take a joke or a punch too well.

Lynn is Irish. It used to be O'Lynn, but Grandpa Bullshit's grandfather dropped the O. In truth, you don't know for sure who your grandfather is. You know who Mom called her father. You also know guys get male pattern baldness from their mother's father, and Grandpa Bullshit died at fifty-one with a full head of hair. Your aunt's son is grown and has a full head of hair, too. The same as Grandpa Bullshit. But both Sam and you have this full-on George Costanza thing going on. A reverse mohawk. Grandpa Bullshit has an illegitimate child. A daughter. It's a safe bet her sons have never pored over the instructions on the back of a bottle of Rogaine. It's a safe bet Grandma Lynn had an illegitimate child too. Let's call her "Mom."

Grandma Lynn and Grandpa Bullshit tried for Mom for a good long while.

Any child, really.

Then her mom gifted her a Kewpie doll as if it'd serve as some sort of sycophantic, creepy, fat, naked, winged, kneeling, praying fertility doll with a single curlicue lock of hair atop its head, looking curiously out of the corner of its eye at some unknown thing.

But it worked.

Grandma Lynn got knockd up right after Great-Grandma gifted her the Kewpie. The little cherub was placed on the nightstand and did its magic. Later, Grandma Lynn gifted the Kewpie to Mom, and—tada—here you are.

It's the only thing Mom left you when she died.

The Kewpie should not be touched unless you want a kid. It should be moved with a pair of salad tongs. No one can really say how that stuff works. Your youngest aunt, the one with the hysterectomy, handles them like an Indian snake charmer. She has a curio cabinet full of them.

Your Kewpie doll isn't kept on the bedside nightstand. The creepy little fucker is enough to make a guy go limp, plus it's a reminder of Mom. And who in their right mind wants to think of their dead mother while they're fucking and trying for a kid? But if you ever do put it to use, it's probably best to fuck with the lights off.

Note to self.

It's a safe bet that's how the other set of grandparents, the ones who raised you, Grandma Audrey and Grandpa Bub, always did it, right? They never lived alone. They always had your big sister, Debbie, and later you under their roof. Grandpa Bub lets out his customary huff of disappointment at everything Dad does and says he does. Grandpa Bub sits silently on the couch, uncrosses his legs, crosses them again, and turns to stare out the window, ignoring Dad, hoping he'll go away, knowing he never will.

Grandpa Bub won't say it to Dad's face, his customary catchphrase he says whenever something burrows beneath his skin, but you know he wants to. You want him to, and in the monotone flatness he uses whenever he wants to joke without coming off as an asshole—the same way he does when the high school lets out and the parade of fatherless, longhaired head-bangers and punks with green and purple mohawks walks by the house.

He stands in the middle of the bay window with his hands on his hips, shaking his head from side to side until the last one trickles by. Grandma Audrey yells at him, "Bub, they can see you!"

He ignores her, says, "If that were my kid, I'd flush it down the toilet," and, later, "If you tell me what it is, I'll tell you what to feed it."

He's not Dad's dad. He never fathered any children. He was a virgin until marriage. He was something like fifty years old when he married Grandma Audrey.

When Debbie gets old enough to take Grandma Audrey out drinking to Charlie's Bar—before it burned and turned into a sodden field where other old ladies take their little kick-me dogs to shit before heading into the vet's office—she learns a life lesson no one should ever get from an elder.

"What's this you got me drinking?" Grandma asks.

"Sex on the Beach, Gram."

"Best damn sex I've had in…twenty years," she says, smacking her lips. "Your Grandpa Bub could fuck a wrinkle all night long and never know the difference."

She orders another, drinks it, waits until it touches her soul before she tells Debbie how she met her first husband, Grandpa Gene, at a fishbowl party. For the uninitiated, a fishbowl party is where the guys put their car keys in a fishbowl and the girls leave with whoever the keys belong to. That was before he left for the Second World War.

But she backs up a little bit and mentions how she first remembers seeing him at a bowling alley on a league night. A girlfriend of hers was so bold as to brag how no woman could take her Gene away. Grandma got him and got a ring from him. But he wasn't the only one who gave her an engagement ring. She got engaged to two soldiers and married the one who made it back. Grandma got pregnant with Dad almost as soon as Grandpa Gene came home. Aunt Bobbie came the year after.

Debbie found Grandpa Gene dead on the shitter about six years before you came to be, so the six-foot-six-inch Swede perched on the living room couch tethered to an oxygen machine is the only one you ever get to call Grandpa. Even though you should call him Granddad, seeing as how it's him who raises you.

POSITIVE & NEGATIVE

YOUR DAD IS A DICK. How that became a nickname for Richard, you'll never understand. Rick makes sense, not Dick.

But he is a dick.

He's bought dream catchers made in Malaysia, for Chrissake. When asked, he tells people he's a Fugawi Indian. If they don't get the joke, he puts a hand to his forehead to block out the sun, leans forward, pretends to squint off into the distance, and says, "Where the Fugawi?" in his best Tonto voice.

The internet will tell you the Fugawi are a nomadic tribe that gets lost a lot.

That makes sense, too.

From Dad, you're Shinnob and Sámi and Innu Montagnais—a little Irish too—which makes you the human equivalent of the swamp water Debbie formulates from the pop machine at the Bonanza all-you-can-eat buffet once you tell her you don't care what she gets you to drink, so she decides it'll be a splash of everything: Coke, Diet Coke, Sprite, Minute Maid, Dr. Pepper, and Hi-C. You wouldn't dare waste it. Waste Grandma's money, and she'll haul you out to the parking lot so fast it'll make your head spin.

Dad put a trailer on a piece of leased land somewhere on the Fond du Lac Indian Reservation, but he isn't enrolled. He doesn't have the pedigree for that. His grandparents attended boarding schools. Neither of them ever stepped foot on a reservation again or told their children anything about being Indian. No creation stories nor tales of Wenaboozhoo. He's like Jack Frost for white people—people like Mom.

An Anishinaabe man took Dad ricing when he was little. Sometimes he points out the spot they went when the two of you motor on over toward the bay. But if you ask him to take you, it's never the right time of year to knock rice. He mutters how he only went once because the two of them flipped the canoe and sank to their knees in loon shit.

Dad drives up to the cabin, points out a field where Indian tobacco grows. But Grandma will have lunch ready, and she'd be upset if it got cold, so you can never stop.

He's never attended ceremony or a single powwow.

He's never smudged nor seen the inside of a sweat lodge.

He's never tied on a single piece of regalia or beadwork.

He's never even worn a ribbon shirt.

He always wears a pair of heavy leather cowboy boots and Wranglers, along with a collared plaid shirt. No one is sure if he does it ironically—dresses like a cowboy—or because he continually listens to country and western songs crooning about sorrow and loss and loneliness.

He never wears a hat, though. He wears everything but the hat. You wear a cowboy hat. It's one of the few things they bought new for you. There's a picture of you sitting on a loveseat with a box of Nilla Wafers and your sister. Your feet are as leathery as his boots, and on your head sits a crushed cowboy hat. Debbie says you never took it off. You even wore it to bed.

Dad takes a deer every fall with a recurve bow—not a compound bow or a rifle, but a recurve bow—the way the real Indians on the television do. He tans the hides himself and hangs them on the wall. After a while, the hides disappear. Whether they get moldy and tossed into the trash or he sells them is anyone's guess.

One afternoon when you come home from school, Grandma Audrey's house looks like a murder scene. The corpse is splayed across the kitchen table with only a blue tarp to catch the blood. Debbie helps him get rid of the body. You help make sausage once you're old enough. He can process a deer all by himself in a single afternoon. He must have taught himself, seeing as how he says Grandpa Gene didn't speak to him until he got old enough to take to a bar and then died five years later.

The first time Dad teaches you anything about being Indian is when he lets you help him under the hood of his car. This time you're not just holding the flashlight for him while he gets upset at something other than you. You're actually helping him hook up his new battery.

He points out the two different posts—positive and negative—and how they each have a corresponding cable. They're impossible to confuse—one barely has enough slack to get to where it needs to, and the other almost falls into place.

Before he hands you the wrench, the battery has to be facing the right direction.

"What's that look like?" he asks.

"A plus sign."

"Mmmhhh, that's the positive. Now, what color is it?"

"Red."

"And the other one?"

"Black."

"What's the little symbol there?" he asks, pointing the handle of the wrench up and down the cable.

"The little line?" you ask. "A takeaway sign?"

"Yeah, it's the negative. Now, does it match up?"

"No," you say, ducking.

"Well, spin the battery around then," he says, stepping back far enough out of the way for you to come out of his shadow.

It's heavier than you imagined, so you take a step closer and press up against the fender, get up on tippy-toes to lift the battery and spin it.

"Don't scratch the paint!" he says. His yelling causes you to duck and stumble and drop the battery. But it lands in place. He pulls the black plastic top off the lead post, shakes it, and asks, "What's this again?"

"The negative."

"That's right, the negative. What's negative mean?"

"Negative's bad."

"That's right. It's black, right? Like a nigger. And they ain't no good either. That's how you remember this and don't fuck up my battery," he says, almost tapping the handle of the wrench against your forehead. "It'll come in handy one day, I promise you."

"Yessir," you say, knowing better than to argue with him regarding how he talks about Black people, knowing it's best to keep quiet and let him say what he will. History has taught you speaking up will only earn you two black eyes.

Then he pulls the red plastic cap off and says, "This is the positive, right? Positive's good. It's red, like us," bringing the cap up to his flushed cheek to illustrate his point.

"Now, put the positive cable on first," he says, handing you the wrench. "You know how you remember that? That the positive goes on first?"

You shake your head from side to side.

"We were here first—and then them cotton-pickers got brought over."

You don't blink or flinch or dare do anything to make him call you some kind of nigger lover. Dad's already mad. You don't dare antagonize him, so you take hold of the cable but let out a whimper and jump back when it crackles and sparks, which makes him laugh and yank the wrench out of your hand.

"Give me that. I'll do it."

You stand back, watch his beet-red face while he ratchets the cables onto the battery.

First the red, then the black.

His lesson in mechanics is what's called a mnemonic device, one of the few he'll ever offer—warped as it is.

Grandma Audrey and Grandpa Gene never taught Dad anything about being Indian because they knew nothing, so he figured out what he could for himself. It's how he became the caricature he is, and how your earliest memory came about: a pack of wolves swarming around you in the living room of a single-wide trailer. That may be a bit of an exaggeration, but to your toddler mind, that's how it felt.

Perhaps a pack of wolves is the wrong way to word it, seeing as how it was a litter of wolf pups. You can keep a wolf as a pet if you live in the city as long as you fence in the yard and you have another fence set up at least thirty-six inches away from the first fence. But you don't live anywhere near the city. The cities on the rez aren't even called towns or townships. They're called villages—at least in Minnesota, on Fond du Lac.

Dad knows of a guy who traps animals and breeds them and sells the offspring to anyone looking for the sort of a pet you can't pick up at the pound. He has bobcats, bear cubs, skunks, and timber wolf pups for sale. His place isn't marked with a road sign cataloging his wares or business hours. Instead, there are a slew of claims about Christ and Commies.

That's where Dad got Brutus.

Brutus isn't entirely weaned, so Mom feeds him from a bottle. One of your bottles. The two of you are only weeks old. He sleeps in your crib, and, later, in the bottom half of the bunk bed with you. You share your home with ferrets and a skunk, too. In the winter, or maybe the early months of spring, Mom keeps chicks and ducklings in the laundry room with a warming light and lines the floor with newspaper. The ducklings and chicks all huddle together around the gravity feeder for warmth. Once, you let a few of the ducklings swim in the toilet bowl until they all drowned from exhaustion. You couldn't have been more than two at the time. Mom giggles when she tells the story about how hard you cried.

Goats and horses are kept out back behind the trailer. Goats for their milk, and horses—because it's what Indians do, right? They kill deer with a bow and arrow and ride horses.

When Mom is pregnant with the two of you, a horse named Regret walks beneath a low-hanging branch to brush her off. Dad gets perturbed and grabs hold of the horse by the bottom jaw, plants his fist between its eyes the way Conan did with a camel. He loves that story. Mom just casts her eyes to the floor and shakes her head, when she confirms the story.

He may have bought Brutus thinking that's how an Indian gets a spirit animal, but Brutus isn't his dog. You're Brutus's human. That's how it works with wolves. Later he brings home Spicy. She isn't his dog either. She's Brutus's mate. They have a litter of pups, which stay in the house until they're weaned. They have the run of the trailer and shadow your every move in hopes you'll lead them to their next meal, as if you're their alpha. But that's not really how being an alpha works. Alphas follow and protect against anything that might threaten the group from the rear. You learn this later, when the Army makes you a sergeant.

Mom is outside hanging clothes on the line when you hear her calling your name, so you grab socks from the dresser drawer and pull a pair of shoes from the depths of the toy box. You know to keep them away from the wolf pups, or else you'll be running around with bare feet.

A few of them tug at your pant legs when you make your way down the hall to the living room, forcing you to high-step to the couch. Still, some of them nip at your toes and the tender bit at the back of the ankle. After climbing up to the relative safety of the couch cushions and slipping on your socks and shoes, you work the laces into rabbit ears. But not fast enough. The tallest of the pups latches onto the loose ends of the laces and tugs on your shoes. The rest of them jump toward you but fall back to the floor, piling on top of one another in a mound of fur and teeth. Before long, they're all taking turns tugging at the toes of the shoes. You yell for Mom, but she's busy or can't hear, so you watch while they pull both shoes off and shred them in a game of tug-of-war. They rip the socks off your feet, too, and you tuck your feet up under your butt, between the couch cushions, while you watch them shred the last pair of matching socks and swallow them on down, elastic and all.

A year later, you watch them do the same to a tiny goat that wiggles its way out of its enclosure and into theirs. A year later, Brutus attacks Dad when he attacks you during a bender. The only thing that saves him is when he thrusts his arm in front of his face and neck. Brutus would have torn out his throat otherwise.

After that, he takes Brutus to the zoo. After that, things get really bad, really quick.

While on a field trip with the pre-K class, you see Brutus behind bars. They keep him and two other timber wolves crammed into a giant aviary where they normally keep owls and eagles that'd lost the gift of flight.

It's a depressing display, and the class loses interest within minutes. The student teacher looks as though she'll shit herself when she urges the class on to the next exhibit and sees you've made your way over the barricade and up to the bars. A thundering growl builds louder and louder in Brutus's chest. Loud enough to keep the other two wolves pinned to the other side of the aviary. You have your arms inside the cage. Your fingers tangle amongst the matted mess of his coat, and you mash your face between the bars while you whisper to him.

You miss your puppy.

Brutus snarls when a zookeeper takes hold of your winter coat and pulls you back to safety. You're still not too talkative and don't dare speak out of turn to an adult, so you let her tell you how dangerous those dogs are. Mom says eventually they sent Brutus out to San Diego to father a few pups, and one day you'll stand outside their square-acre enclosure wondering which ones. Passersby will tell their kids to look at the wolves, and you'll whisper back, "Ma'iingan," correcting them.

When you fly home for her funeral, Mom's brother, Brian, is waiting for you inside his woodshop. He's been waiting all day. He doesn't offer a hello. Instead he asks, "Who the hell raises wolves?" before he hugs you, quaking and crying.

Mom did. She raised wolves. Boys too.

MEDICINE MAN

BREAKFAST IS NOTHING SPECIAL. IT's merely a means of lessening the harshness of the cocktail of pharmaceuticals prescribed to help you make it through the day. You wonder whether they'll fix your head before they destroy your liver and stomach lining. But, still, you take your medicine, a mouthful of pills meant to stop you from giving your Beretta a blowjob. It's simple physics: no two objects can occupy the same space at the same time.

There's one pill, four times a day, to keep your mood stable. No more explosions. No more manic episodes. No more fight or flight or freeze. When the gelcap explodes, when its contents creep back up your esophagus, its acidity flashes you back to the taste the CLP left on your tonsils—right before you remembered it's got to come straight up from under the jaw and back behind your eyeballs on its way to the top of the skull, unless you'd like some CNA at the vet's home to wipe your ass for the rest of your life. And then you lost your nerve, again, and slid the safety back on.

Or maybe they give you a colostomy bag and a catheter these days.

There's another pill for the trip to Africa—a diseased land with diseased water that breeds mosquitoes that'll kill you as quick as anything. Though the pills they gave you to protect you from their bite cause brain damage mimicking the scars of combat, so they throw more pills your way and cut you a bigger disability check.

There's a two-tone brown and beige alpha-blocker you take before bedtime. Your heart is fine, but the pills have a curious side effect of stopping you from dreaming.

No dreams means no nightmares.

There is no bent piece of red willow rounded into a hoop held tight by an interwoven, interlaced net of sinew hanging anywhere in the apartment. Still, this two-tone brown and beige blood pressure pill is your dreamcatcher, and the pharmacist is your medicine man.

He warns they'll make you lightheaded, so you should take some time getting up in the morning. But when you gotta go, you gotta go, and you're getting older now, and you gotta go in the middle of the night sometimes, and one time a girlfriend finds you lying on the bathroom floor. Not dead, but dizzy. Cold, yes. But it is Minnesota. And it's winter. And the basement is not insulated, so it's safe to say the floor is freezing. The house is better than a hundred years old with next to no updates, meaning: there is no exhaust fan, so it gets humid in there when you shower, and it stays humid. The Visqueen keeps falling from the window, and the breeze from the blizzard is blowing the blackout curtains. When she touches your leg to shake you, you feel icy, and she knows this is how your mother was found, so she lets out a scream, one that startles you awake, and you thump your head on the tub you somehow missed when you fell to the floor—along with the toilet and sink. But you learned to sleep where you can ages ago, and sometimes that means sleeping where you fall.

LOVE LEAVES SCARS

Taking these pills or asking for the pills or admitting you can't do it without pills leaves you with the feeling of cottonmouth all on its own. Before the pills, there's talk therapy with the one and only psychologist the VA employs at the local rural clinic. He mentions how he has the same running shoes as you to build rapport and how he got his PhD down in southern Mississippi, where you were stationed for a good chunk of the time you served. You reminisce about the cuisine you miss—Cajun, Creole, soul food—and talk about how nothing pleases your palate anymore. The flavors are dull, the colors are dim, the volume is muted on everything except for the one thing in front of you at that particular moment in time. His expression changes when he realizes you're not talking about chicken and dumplings or split pea soup.

It's at that moment he asks you to recite the five worst moments of your time in war and conflict. "No particular order, just whatever comes to mind first," he says. Then he wants to hear the next one, and the next one, until he has five moments he can discuss with you.

He doesn't get how if you crack the door, it'll become a fatal funnel. He doesn't get how the memories clump together in a Spirograph of a Venn diagram. He has you buy a Walkman with a microphone. Together, you produce a soundtrack your five worst demons can exercise to. They are the moments you haven't managed to repress all the way or convince yourself never happened in the waking world.

The doctor's orders are to go home and listen to the stories you've told him once a day until the next week, when he'll see you again and have you tell the same stories again, like the proverbial resident drunk at the VFW that forgot to go on living after they were handed their discharge papers. The doctor will re-record you and have you listen to the remastered versions of these easy-listening classics. He wants you to build a callus, become numb, have these haunting tales become background noise. So he hears these scattered and abridged tales, the ones that torment you when you dare close your eyes at night. He says the more you discuss, the more that'll be remembered. But that's not how revision works.

The first rule of storytelling is to know the audience. The more of an encore he asks for, the more likely it is that you'll word it in a way that makes the most sense to someone such as him, who's only watched a handful of war flicks or studied the aftereffects in a textbook or watched someone else poke and prod some other lab rat from behind a two-way mirror. The story won't be free-flowing. Words will have to be measured. Still, if you don't play his game, he can tell them you don't need or want their help and then they'll have a reason to take away your benefits, pull the rug out from underneath you so you can slip through the crack and save Uncle Sam some money, leave you to twist in the wind—dance a jig—join the daily twenty-two.

This becomes Mad Libs with fractured frightening details outlining a day in the life of a man who's paid to die in the name of God and country and cheap foreign crude oil, yet doesn't. It's all one nightmare, whether you're asleep or no.

Your eyes fixate on the filigreed piece of parchment he's tacked to the wall above his desk while you talk about waking to VBIEDs exploding less than a football field away from the tent, sleeping through others, and the accompanying small arms attacks. You tell him about taking fire in a Blackhawk. You talk about being shelled from the MSR while taking a lap around the track. You talk about maneuvering down Enterprise Drive, a car T-boning the Humvee and watching the gunner shatter the windshield and the bones of the overzealous bastard sitting behind the steering wheel, followed by you pouring out the door once you get inside the serpentine and puking into the roasting sand. You talk about when a Kurd locks you in with forty detainees and emotions you still cannot define and how those images come back every time you close your eyes and how every time you open your mouth after that, you have fewer bits of teeth. You talk about waiting month after month for luck to end, but it never does, so you go on waiting to die, and you are still waiting.

He takes note of how your teeth grit when you tell these stories. He surmises you don't want to tell them. You're bearing down so hard on your back teeth it doesn't even look like your mouth is moving. It's almost as if telling these stories is a kind of ventriloquism. Your teeth grind this way and that until they slide into an overbite and stay that way, giving you the inflection of a bulldog who growls when he means to say hello.

He won't hear about you shuffling into a trailer half-asleep—a makeshift latrine—at 3 a.m. and finding an escaped detainee. He won't hear about you beating the guy senseless until you come back to yourself and remember where you are and that you're on R&R, and this man, who is only trying to clean the shitters, doesn't say a thing because he has a family to feed. At least that's what makes the most sense.

He won't hear about exploding out of your bed and tackling some Lieuy who shook you awake when you needed to go talk to the TOC, so they could tell you what you could and could not say about the Blackhawk taking fire because Blackhawks can't take fire in the Green Zone. If attacks happen there, then it wouldn't be a Green Zone, understand?

He won't hear about working an intake detail and having a detainee stand like the Vitruvian Man, finding a Wahabi tattoo on his hand—a dagger with wings—when you roll his wrist skyward, looking at his face, finding his face looks far too much like your father's, putting him in a wristlock, forcing him to the floor, down onto his knees—in terrible pain, crying the way Dad did the last time you saw him at Deb's house during Christmas, when he said he could still kick your ass, so you made him cry out, too, "David, you're hurting me. Please stop." But you don't stop until everyone hears and everyone comes to see for themselves. Aunt Bobbie comes out of the kitchen, and the cousins come inside the house, and your nephew stands back far enough to take in the spectacle of it all.

But this man you have by the wrist isn't Dad. He's some bloated terrorist with a scraggly black beard, all of which leaves him looking like Bluto.

After the fifth week, the shrink says it'll get worse before it gets better. On the sixth week, the doctor says he's making you worse, he's not helping you, and asks, "What therapy do you think would help? What therapy do you want to try?" You ask, "Which one of us has a PhD?" and add an oh-by-the-way, telling him how you went to the USM library last time you visited Mississippi. You read his dissertation—at least the abstract. He stutters through the rest of the conversation in defeat, says he'll see you once a month instead of once a week.

Once a month happens only once.

Before the talk therapy, there is the church. You don't know who has your back, who you can trust, so maybe it's time for omniscience. No one says where to be and when to be there or what to do but you, and you begin to think more and more how fellating your .40 caliber S&W doesn't sound like such a bad idea. You have no faith in His words or comfort in His house, but you've witnessed enough monstrosities and atrocities to entertain the idea of ever-after evils actually existing. That alone is enough to convince almost anyone to sit in a pew and listen until they too are a lost little sheep, confused as to what it is they can and cannot do—so they resign to life on their knees. The church limps along, leaning on blind obedience, but you've learned blind obedience tends to get guys killed when the guy behind the podium has never stepped foot into the valley of the shadow of death, and he's talking about being God-fearing. Fearing God, in other words. Fearing breaking His rules, and He has rules against everything and everything is an abomination, but only some of the abominations are brought into the light. Questions are met with the same look you got back in the fourth grade from Mrs. McClaire, who taught Monday through Friday in one classroom and in another come Sunday mornings. She teaches you about Abraham and all his children, but when you ask her, "What about Tad?" to prove you were paying attention to her in her other class, it's safe to say she gets more than a tad perturbed with you and asks you to sit in the church with the adults until it's time for the kids' choir practice.

You don't argue because she's good friends with Grandma Audrey. Tomorrow is Monday, so you'll see Mrs. McClaire then too. If you don't go sit with the adults, there's a good possibility your desk will be sitting in the corner under her blackboard all by itself come Monday morning, or else right next to her desk, so you can't disturb the rest of her class with your questions.

The kids' choir practice plays out like a broken record. There's only one boy with a baritone voice, and later a bass. And that's you. So, guess who always plays Joseph and is always at center stage when it comes time for solos during the Christmas and Easter pageants. Because of this, older girls forget how young you really are. Because of this, you are a bit naïve when it comes to matters of the heart. And there's not a whole lot more frustrating for a girl in grade school than unrequited love.

This one little blonde girl pushes you when you don't even look her way while she's flirting. Not that you're all that aware of what flirting entails.

She knocks you off balance and into one of the metal folding chairs. It's innocent flirting. But when a human head slams into a metal folding chair, the metal hinge slams shut without hesitation or protest. It is what the manufacturer meant to happen when the seat and backrest are shoved toward one another with enough force, after all.

After all this time, there's no knowing who separated the eyebrow from the metal hinge of the chair, but it's a safe bet it was done as a reflex. What is still fresh in your memory, however, is how everyone stared at the hand you held right against the source of the searing pain.

The kids' choir director's requests to see what was hidden beneath that hand were ignored until the pain subsided enough for you to pay attention to something else. The sight of the glob of blood on its way down to the floor proved as captivating for you as it is indelible.

Blood really does fall in slow motion.

The sweet little blonde girl who caused all of this to happen scurried over to the wastebasket and retched in regret or disgust. Who's to say? The two of you never again spoke. But the church loves to tell you how love is patient, love is kind, love does not envy, love does not boast, love is not proud, love does not dishonor others, love is not self-seeking, love is not easily angered, love keeps no record of wrongs, love does not delight in evil but rejoices with the truth, love always protects, it always trusts, always hopes, always perseveres, it never fails. Where there are prophecies, they will cease; where there are tongues, they will be stilled; where there is knowledge, it will pass away. But it fails to mention how unrequited love leaves scars.

THE ART OF PREMEDITATION

OF ALL THE IMAGES AND smells and sounds that burrowed into the limbic system, there's not one memory of Mom and Dad as man and wife.

Grandma Audrey says, "You're making that up," or "That's your imagination playing tricks on you," or simply, "That never happened," atop her saying how Mom is dead and gone whenever she's asked to confirm something you remember about your life back before you came to live at her house, back when you were little.

There's only one remaining picture of the wedding. It's not of them standing before a preacher bookended by the best man and maid of honor, but of Mom sitting on the Davenport in Grandma Audrey's living room between Grandpa Bub and Grandpa Bullshit. Mom is a petite little thing wearing a white wispy-looking dress with muted green trim—an overlap of hippie and disco fashion. It's her second wedding, too, so it's an off-white dress. She's about six months pregnant, but no one would know by the way the dress fits her frame.

Dad is off-camera somewhere, dressed in a Key lime–colored leisure suit.

Grandpa Bub has squished himself up against the far end of the Davenport and stares off into the middle distance. There's plenty of room for the three of them, but he's doing all he can to cushion himself from this shotgun wedding.

Grandpa Bullshit leans as far forward as he can in the hopes of getting out of frame, but his buzz cut and burning cigarette are in sharp focus.

The only picture of Mom and Dad while they're married is one of them sitting on that same olive-drab Davenport with you three months later. You can't be more than a couple of days old. Mom's in a T-shirt proclaiming "What You See Is What You Get," and Dad's dressed in a pair of black and blue and gray plaid bell bottoms, along with a white short-sleeve shirt with a butterfly collar.

He hasn't buttoned his shirt and looks like an Indian Tony Manero. He's smiling, but not at the camera. He's got his arm around Mom and his eyes glued to you, his only begotten son. Mom, though, she's posed, sitting up straight, holding you up for whoever is behind the camera, smiling ear to ear. Her whiteness—your whiteness—never dawns on you until it is placed alongside his Indianness.

Dad's been divorced for most of your life and sparsely dated. There is one time during junior high when you crawl into his car and catch a whiff of something. In the backseat lies a crumpled mess a little too lacy to belong to either of you two. Curiosity gets in the way of better judgment, and you find yourself pinching a pair of panties.

Dad says, "Hmm, where'd those come from?" with a laugh.

You say, "Where'd that come from?" pointing to the half-smoked joint in the ashtray, but he doesn't answer. He just lets out the clutch and drives down the alleyway.

Before whoever forgot her panties, there was Connie. They dated for several years, but she stopped coming around right after you turned five, right after she bought you this massive folding case full of Crayola water paints, crayons, Cray-Pas, colored pencils, markers—sixty-four of each.

More than that, for a time, Connie made you feel like you had a mom.

The last image you have of her is when she and her sister Donna, along with Aunt Bobbie and Auntie Harriet and Grandma Audrey and Debbie, all sat around the dining room table, clucking, talking bad about men.

You do your best to ignore them and their girl talk. When you grow weary of being excluded from the conversation because you're a boy, you say something about how you don't want to be a man when you grow up, which makes them all cackle. No one likes getting laughed at, so you sprawl out on the carpet with a bunch of construction paper and all those colors and create. But "If you're going to eavesdrop, pay attention." At least that's what Grandma Audrey always said.

Connie's dating Dad, and Grandma's got Grandpa Bub. Auntie Harriet has henpecked the hell out of Uncle Harold. Aunt Bobbie's fine without a man, but Donna does have man problems.

Her husband, Steve, is a mailman, but he's not the proverbial mailman with a bunch of kids living along his route who look suspiciously like him. Donna's problem arises from the recent discovery of how Steve has been inappropriate with her daughters since right after they got married. Her oldest won't talk. She cries when you ask her what's wrong. It was her youngest who told Donna what was happening.

Someone says something about cutting off his tallywacker.

Someone else shakes their head and says she has to kill the bastard.

Connie agrees and asks, "How?"

Shoot him, plain and simple, is the consensus of the table.

Take a gun and shoot him.

Connie says something about ambushing him along his mail route while it's still dark out and shooting him in the chest.

Grandma says there's no way you could sneak up on a man who walks the same route every single day. Men are already paranoid as can be. She could never walk up behind her Gene without him getting spooked even while he was relaxing in the recliner.

Then the table gets a bit more creative.

Then they get really specific.

Then Grandma says they got to stop talking about it. It's gone from a bunch of hypotheticals to premeditation. She crushes out her cigarette, leans back in her chair, folds her arms. Connie says they have to get going anyway.

Steve was killed on April 4, 1982.

Donna found a guy at the Red Lion Bar who agreed to do it for five hundred dollars—let's call him Todd. She knew the guy. She was a regular, as was he. As was Dad. Steve wasn't. Todd didn't know Donna's husband; he only knew Steve was a child-molesting mailman. He didn't need to know much else, but, still, Donna added a little more to the story every time she reintroduced the subject.

She even wrote down her husband's work schedule and the license plate numbers for the vehicles he drove.

Todd told her he'd think about it.

Two hours passed, and Todd had heard enough, told Donna to drive him home where he'd change clothes. Then he asked if she would be so kind as to bring him up to the Bridgeman's restaurant across the street from the bowling alley. He'd handle things from there.

Todd waited for Steve in the parking lot by his vehicle, asked if he could hitch a ride. Steve agreed, since Todd's place was along the way.

Todd shot Steve in the chest a total of five times, dumped his body, drove his Jeep back to the bowling alley, called Donna from a payphone, told her to come to get him, but grew antsy and walked to her house instead. From there, the two of them went down to the Aerial Lift Bridge and parked in its shadow to talk about what happened before he took off for Texas.

Donna was convicted of first-degree murder for her involvement in her husband's death. Todd did time, too, of course.

A week after the trial, Connie told Donna's attorney it was her who set the whole thing up—not her sister. She never even let her sister know what she had planned.

Donna was innocent. Oblivious.

The attorney taped the conversation, which contradicted her testimony at the earlier trial. Guilt-ridden, she admitted to lying under oath and talking her sister into lying too.

Come Connie's trial, she pleaded the Fifth. Donna sang. She talked about how they rehearsed what to say so much that they had a running bet concerning the verdict. Connie pleaded guilty to perjury and conspiring to mislead the jury. The court concluded anyone aware of the things Steve did to Donna's girls had reason to fabricate a fictional version of what they knew about his demise—including Connie's lover—which is how the court officially referred to Dad.

He never dated again.

He didn't know how to take the fact that the woman he loved used all the other women he loved as a think tank to come up with a way to kill off his child-molesting brother-in-law. It was a bit too much for him to wrap his head around. He stayed single, hoarded VHS tapes with unending hours of bootleg porn, and drank. The only pictures of women he kept around were printed on shiny paper and unfolded from the center of some magazine.

MULTIPURPOSE CLEANER

YOUR FIRST MEMORY IS NOT when the wolf pups bit at your ankles and pulled the socks and shoes from your feet. If you close your eyes, shuffle through all those little flits and flashes from childhood, it'll dawn on you how that very first memory involved Grandma Lynn, Grandpa Bullshit, and the Pillsbury Doughboy. The whole scene takes all of ten seconds.

While toddling around her kitchen, out of curiosity you wander over to her to see what she is doing. Someone working quietly draws you in like the hypnotic blue light of a bug zapper. You stop inches from her butt—right as she bangs a can of biscuits against the edge of the counter hard enough for them to burst open on the first try. You're in diapers still, which is fortunate, because you fall to the floor, cheeks first, and wail. It's your own fault for walking around like a cat all the time, anyway. But you do so because Dad's head is sensitive to sound once he finds his way home, so like a doting son you learn to tiptoe around the trailer to not disturb his beauty sleep. But even that's not exactly foolproof, so Mom plops you down into the playpen, where you sit hunched against the screen mesh until lunchtime, and then dinner time, and then bedtime, until the doctor says you have a curvature of the spine.

Your crying on the kitchen floor gets drowned out by Grandpa Bullshit's laughing. He sits and watches the whole thing play out. He knows what's coming, and he thinks it'll be funny as all hell and wouldn't dare spoil it for himself by uttering a word of warning. His laugh turns to a cough, which turns to phlegm rising, so he makes his way to the spittoon beside his bed.

That would be the same spittoon Mom talks about in another story, about you acting out at her parents' house because you can't at your parents' house. She found you laughing, giggling, playing in their bedroom, jumping on their springy double bed. Instead of breaking your neck, you bounce all over until you slide off the edge and land feet first into the spittoon, where your knees fold and you sink to your chin, and the cup overfloweth.

Mom gags and lets go a shiver when she tells you this part of the story.

While she cleans her father's phlegm out of your hair and from between your toes and the creases of your chubby little legs, you can't stop giggling. It tickles you and sickens her each time her fingers find another glob of her father's phlegm caked in some hidden crease. It eventually becomes too much for her to handle and she pukes all over you.

The shower is raining down, causing you to slide this way and that, all across the tub in every imaginable direction. You are still laughing, giggling, having a grand ol' time, while she's grabbing for you, trying to get hold of you, and getting sicker each time she touches you. This last small detail sticks with you once you remember how Mom said she never wanted kids; she only wanted out of her parents' house.

Flash forward to the summer before you turned four, the first summer after you went to stay with Grandma Audrey, the summer you got into the bucket of tar when someone forgot to snap the lid down tight after they'd finished fixing the leaky roof.

It's summer, so it's hot out, so you are in a pair of tighty-whities because they are just as good as swim trunks, so the tar gets everywhere. You try to run to the lake and wash it off, but, like a good dog, Scrappy won't let you go more than knee-deep out into the lake. The downside of Scrappy's heroism is that it allows Grandma Audrey to get a hold of you. She's always been what could best be called a take-action kind of gal, so she won't wait for the tar to dry and peel it carefully away from the skin. Instead, she sits you in a plastic tub in the sink and puts a kettle on the stove.

The tar comes off easily enough for her with some scalding hot water and a Brillo pad. Debbie scrambles into the kitchen when she hears you scream. No one ever knew what Grandma was doing until she was already doing it, and there is no way to stop her, even when Debbie's screaming joins in a duet with yours.

Screaming does nothing but make Debbie sick and puke on herself a little. Once she's able to catch her breath, she runs off into the woods beside the cabin and hides in the tree fort she and some of the big cousins built. There she stays until your crying can no longer be heard coming from the cabin's kitchen window.

There are no witnesses who can say how long it took for the tar to come off, or if Grandma Audrey took breaks, or if your tears caused her any tears. No one stuck around to witness the scene, save the green ceramic frog that sat speechless on the side of the sink with mouth agape.

That must have been the summer of 1981.

DEBBIE DO

A ROOSTER CROWS ITS COCK-A-DOODLE-DO and wakes the wolves and the dogs, setting off a chorus of howls and yelps and barking, which makes Dad belt out, "Shut the fuck up!" at the top of his lungs because he believes doing so will silence the animals and not startle those of the children who managed to sleep through the sounds of the waking zoo that is your childhood home.

Mom's voice clamors down the hallway of the trailer, yelling back a simple, "Fuck you, Richard!" followed by her cackling like a witch, as if he's too hungover to rise from the recliner and retaliate.

The only answer to Mom's outburst is the sound of some falling birdseed and the clank of Charlie's metal ankle bracelet against the bars of his aviary when he hops from his perch to the side of his cage, making the most racket he can.

His flight feathers have grown back again.

Your big sister, Debbie, is the oldest of you kids but scared to death of him. She's not going to let him out; she's too busy taking care of you and watching Sam.

She gave you a bottle at noon—like she was told to do—but Dad's ferret took it out of the crib, again, and hid beneath the recliner, again. Historically, he attacks anyone who gets too close or tries to retrieve it, so Debbie sits cross-legged alongside Sam on the couch, where they share a box of King Vitamin cereal and watch an episode of *Captain Kangaroo*.

Flower, Debbie's skunk, curls up next to her, along with one of the cats, the one that can't meow anymore since Dad sent it flying into the screen door when it tripped him one time too many. With her one hand, she takes turns petting the two. With her other hand, she reaches toward the bottom of the box of King Vitamin to find Sam's left nothing but dust.

You kids are all right by yourselves as long as Charlie keeps up his impressions of Mom and Dad yelling at one another. A passerby would never know there are no adults home.

As if on cue, Charlie screams, "Dammit, David!" sounding every bit like Mom. It's a nudge for Debbie to check on you. Charlie likes to snitch when you make it out of the crib. He's not the only help she has—Brutus makes a nest of the baby-blue, blue-ribbon-winning afghan Aunt Bobbie crocheted, and lies on the floor between you kids and the front door. But this is back when you lived on a dead-end road on the outer edge of the rez—not a bad neighborhood where some questionable character can come knocking at any given moment.

Debbie is ten-ish, and already well-versed in temporary living conditions as well as taking care of herself. She wasn't even a year old when her mom left Dad. The next day, he brought Debbie to Aunt Bobbie, and Grandma Audrey took over following the news about her mother dying in a head-on collision somewhere in Kansas. Somewhere is still all anyone knows. Grandma Audrey is the only mother Debbie can call to mind.

Grandma Audrey doted on Debbie when she was little, even when they would argue, and she'd say, "Debbie, don't." Debbie would counter her with a concise "Debbie, do!" and both would laugh.

Your mom is only twelve years older than Debbie—still technically a teenager—so Debbie doesn't like listening to her. But she won't have to for long. She'll leave for Grandma's house again right after Mom takes you and Sam and goes into hiding.

She will grow weary of Dad's disappearing acts and his mistaking her for a punching bag when he magically reappears. Luckily, like most bullies, all she'll have to do is hit him once for him to stop. She'll take hold of his leather Brunswick bag and slap him in the ear. For extra credit, she'll neglect to remove the bowling ball beforehand. This is what she means when she says, "Hell hath no wrath like when your mother really gets pissed off."

Debbie won't go back to Grandma's house after that, but will find herself living under the roof of Grandma's second husband, Grandpa Bub. Leroy is his legal name.

You will go there to live, too, a little less than a year later.

Debbie's superpower is saving you from Grandma's split pea soup by saying she wants mac and cheese with hot dogs for dinner instead. If you said something of the sort, Grandma would fire back with, "What do you think this is, a goddamned restaurant?" and punctuate it with a backhand swing if you were within her wingspan. But Debbie can get away with it. Partially because she is old enough to make it for herself and partially because she is a girl and Grandma raised boys and girls with entirely opposite approaches.

Grandpa and Grandma finish off the split pea soup without complaint, but they did both survive the Depression, so it almost serves as comfort food. Grandpa Bub also puts his bowl down by his feet, where the dogs congregate, once Grandma excuses herself from the table.

In exchange, you save Debbie from Grandma finding her extra pack of cigarettes while she is at school. You can hide things a whole lot better than Debbie. That's the end result of being too strict with a kid: they become sneaky. They learn how to construct a plausible lie; they learn to think ten steps ahead, to think of every conceivable scenario both logical and illogical before they ever act or open their mouths to answer a question. They never stop playing the what-if game.

Grandpa Bub's house is old. Come springtime, it rains a lot. The ground is already soft from all the snowmelt, so the house shifts some. On one rainy afternoon, Grandma hears a stack of pots and pans fall inside the cupboard between the stove and the fridge. After she investigates the scene of this most heinous crime, she calls you downstairs and waits for you in the kitchen with her arms folded, tapping her toes on the floor—almost pointing them at what's got her pissed.

"Why'd you stack them like that?" When you look to see what she is talking about, you don't answer. You try to fix it, make it right. "I don't want you to fix it," she says, swatting you in the head, so you come out of the cabinet and look up at her from the floor. "I asked you why you stacked them that way. If I've shown you once, I've shown you a million times how to stack them, now haven't I?"

This is a crime you didn't commit, and when you tell her so, she stoops down and grabs you by the collar and warns you, "Don't lie."

It's not a lie, you tell her. You promise.

"Those pots and pans?" she asks. "You didn't stack *those* pots and pans?" she says again and reaches a hand into the cabinet.

"No, Grandma, no."

"Don't you tell me no."

She beats you for lying to her, and when she gets so winded she needs a break, you confess to the crime, defeated. You lie about lying. You want her to stop and you want her to be happy to have you as a helper. You want her to trust you, too.

But by telling her you did it, that you didn't do as she said when she showed you how to stack the pots and pans a million times, and that you lied about ignoring her instructions—she becomes reinvigorated. All you can do is wrap your hands around your head and bury your face and chin into your chest and wait for it to be over.

If memory serves, this all took place around 3:30 in the afternoon, because that's when Debbie comes in from school and is greeted by the sight of Grandma cracking you with a saucepan over and again, and she says, "No, Grandma, no!"

She wants to know what you did this time. Grandma says you stacked the pots and pans wrong, and they tipped over, and now the whole cupboard is a mess. Debbie says, "He didn't put away the dishes last. I did."

Grandma lets go of your shirt collar and tells Debbie, "You shouldn't stack them like that, you know better. You know how they go."

Deflated, Grandma hands you the saucepan she's been swinging and tells you to put it away—the right way. Debbie, down on the floor on her hands and knees, helps you put them away, whispering "Sorry, sorry" more times than you can count.

Sometimes it's torturous to have a sister a decade older than you. Debbie finds it funny to straddle you and pound her pointer finger into your sternum, forcing you to laugh until it's impossible to breathe, until it's impossible to hold it in any longer. She hollers out, "David peed on me," and Dad yells back, "Bet you won't do that again."

He's right. She won't. She'll pick on you one day and beat up someone else who does the same the next. The Miller kid, across the street, sticks you up on top of a garage roof for flicking him off, and Debbie gives him a bloody nose for being mean to her little brother. Your broomball coach busts your teeth during practice, and Debbie throws her a blanket party. Debbie sees Grandma has you cornered in the bathroom, demanding to know the name of the centerfold model in the foldout you hid behind the radiator, and Debbie tells her, "It's from a girlie magazine, he wouldn't know. How would he know her name?"

Still, Grandma's question needs an answer, so you open it up to read the woman's name aloud until it becomes obvious no one is listening, they're too busy arguing amongst themselves. Grandma is too upset by it all and tells Debbie, "You deal with him."

Debbie chases you down the hallway, calling you a pervert, laughing, bouncing around in a boxer's stance. When she swings, so do you, and she screams, "David broke my hand!"

Grandma yells back, "Good God, what now?"

Debbie tells her, "I tried to hit him."

That hand turned so green, and swelled so fast, you swore Debbie was secretly She-Hulk.

A few short weeks after, she showed up at Dad's front door. When he opened it, she told him, "I ran away from home."

"You are home," he said, and unlatched the storm door.

Debbie might not have been at Grandma's house to protect you anymore, but it should never have been her job anyway.

FORCED ENTRY

REMEMBER YOUR FIRST GIRLFRIEND?

Not the forbidden love you hide away from the world because she is in the first grade and you are in kindergarten but still only weeks apart in age. Your bedroom looks across the alley into hers, and seeing her silhouette move from one window to the other makes being grounded in your room seem less lonely.

Not one of the girls you walk with on the way home from school because there aren't any boys in your grade who live on your block.

Not the girl who walks three blocks and waits outside every evening while you eat dinner, and Debbie sings, "Your girlfriend's here." You blush and grit your teeth and growl, "She's not my girlfriend." But you'd like her to be. There's something about her impossibly blue eyes and her black hair she cannot cut and the denim dresses that stop at the ankle and the collared shirts she cannot change out of no matter how hot the summer sun gets.

Not the first girl you see naked. She keeps telling you not to look while she changes into her swimsuit beneath the deck in the backyard of her parents' house. It's not like you know what to look for, and this happens long before you notice she even is a girl—back before you understand the difference between boys and girls.

Not even the first girl to hold your hand and kiss you on the lips and call you her boyfriend, even if it is only when she comes to see her mom every other weekend the summer before seventh grade.

No, this girl is the first girl to go out with you on a date. A real date. The two of you take the city bus downtown and transfer up to the mall. She sneaks you into your first R-rated film and nudges you toward the center seat of the back row. You can't remember what movie it was. She shoves her tongue down your throat and guides your hand up her shirt and under her bra and whispers into your ear how she wants you to tease, twist, tug, and pinch her nipples. She wants anything but gentle. When you finally get it right, she unzips you and snakes her hand through the flaps in the front of your boxers and gives you your first handjob.

She yanks on it.

She's touching your penis, but handling it the way you handle the joystick when you get down to your last guy on *Yars' Revenge*. It doesn't feel good until it does, and then you explode all over her hand and inside your boxers, and that doesn't happen again until boot camp, when you wake with your sweatpants stuck to your thighs, and the fire watch says you were jacking off and snoring at the same time. They don't stop laughing until you ask why they would stand there watching you jerk off and then loiter while you lie satisfied in the afterglow.

But this girl, man—this is the girl who trounces other girls for leaving notes in your locker and pulls a knife on you when you tell her you're moving to your mom's house on the other side of town for high school. She says, "No, you're not," and you plant your size ten into her gut and grab the knife. No one says anything to any teachers, so neither of you gets detention. Besides, the two of you are holding hands on the way to your next class, anyhow.

At thirteen, she has the curves and the endowments you know a woman is supposed to have, courtesy of the French nudes featured in Grandma's Time-Life books. But the insides of her forearms look like the etched walls of a prison cell, each individual cut counting the days of her hell. See, her dad is a gambler and a drinker. And he hosts poker night. And he can't hold his liquor. And he gets blackout drunk every single time. His buddies leave him where he falls.

One evening she wakes with one of them on top of her, inside of her. Then they all take a turn. When she tells him, her father, a cop, he won't believe her. She'd been bitching about how loud they were and how tomorrow was a school day and how she wanted them all to leave. They were, all of them, cops.

It was forced entry.

Nothing happens to them, so it happens to her again and again and again until she loses count. You're the only one who'll listen to her. The only one who'll let her tell her story.

She says all of this in a drunken stupor. She's not old enough to buy alcohol. She's not even old enough to drive. She never gets old enough to buy alcohol for herself. Her father finds her hanging before that can happen. She told him what they did to her one last time. She wrote it all down this time. She would not be interrupted this time.

Yeah, that girlfriend. Let's not forget her.

YOU THINK THIS IS A JOKE

THREE GUYS WALK INTO A bar: a cowboy, an Indian, and this Black guy. It's a dingy, dimly lit dump of a place. Dad doesn't give much more detail than that, but it matches every bar he's brought you into, so the setup is believable.

They all belly up to the bar and order a drink. The cowboy orders a glass of Colorado Kool-Aid. The Indian and the Black guy ask the bartender to line up a few shots for them. While the cowboy sips away at his beer and watches the television above the bar, the Indian hoists the first shot glass into the air and says, "Once we were many, now we are few," in a flat and somber tone, before slamming a mouthful of whiskey and swallowing hard.

While the Indian exhales a long, slow breath, the Black guy nods and snatches up one of the shot glasses and says, "Once we were few, now we are many!"

The cowboy clears his throat, itches his nose, sniffs, leans forward, looks down the bar and says, "That's because we haven't played Cowboys and Negroes yet."

Dad knows no other way to teach you about the loss your ancestors endured.

There's this big Hollywood production company filming a movie about outer space in the desert. A week into production, an old Indian man walks into the middle of the set while they're shooting an action scene on the desertscape. The instant the director notices him, he yells, "Cut!"

All the actors go silent and stare at the old Indian man, who looks at the director, realizing he is the man in charge, and says, "You go, rain come. Make big flood."

The director laughs and others join in. Security escorts the old Indian man off camera.

Half an hour passes, and the sky goes black. The director loses his light, so filming is done for the day. The actors retreat to their trailers. Then the rain comes, and a flash flood washes across the desert, destroying the movie set.

Everyone goes back to wherever they call home.

Six months later, the film finds new investors and the director brings his cast and crew back out into the desert. This time they decide to shoot the film in the driest days of summer.

Once again, a week of filming passes, and the old Indian man walks into the middle of all the action. He stands in front of the camera and says, "You go, ice fall from sky. Break camera. Break everything."

Once again, the director yells, "Cut!" from behind the monitor and calls security to escort the old Indian man off the set. But the laughter is enough to make him leave on his own.

Half an hour later, hail the size of golf balls falls from the sky. They grow bigger and bigger the longer the storm continues—some the size of grapefruits, even. A couple of the actors are injured before they can retreat to their trailers. The lights and the cameras are all destroyed. The set looks like Swiss cheese.

Defeated, the director returns to Hollywood.

A year later, behind schedule and way over budget, the director, cast, and crew come back to the desert. This time, however, before the first day of filming, the director sends security to find the old Indian man, which takes a day or two, but they do find him, and they do bring him to the set. The director says to the old Indian man, "Chief, I want to offer you a job. Do you want a job?"

"Yah," the old Indian man says. "Course."

"Okay," says the director. "Tell me, what's the weather going to do?"

"Don't know," says the old Indian man. "Radio broke."

Dad knows no other way to teach you Indians aren't magical or mystical, despite what the TV and the teacher who made you read *The Indian in the Cupboard* taught you.

A group of friends want to go out West and hunt buffalo. They find a brochure saying there must be at least four in the group, not including their guide. And they must hunt on horseback. They all want the authentic experience, so they hire an Indian guide.

He comes cheap, he travels light. He doesn't even need a saddle.

He takes them across the prairie, talks about how much meat each man will get for their families, how the hide can be used to keep them warm and clothed, turned into moccasins, tipis, blankets, leather for saddles, how the bones can be carved to make knives or boiled to make glue, even the scrotum can be turned into a canteen for carrying water, how the horns and hooves can be used to drink from, how the sinew should not be wasted—even in today's world. But they see no buffalo their first day and decide to make camp for the night.

The hunters complain to their guide, and he tells them about Buffalo Bill Cody killing millions of buffalo during the days of the Medicine Lodge Treaty, the treaty they used to put the Plains Indians onto reservations.

They're hunting the offspring of the few survivors.

The following morning, they ride along the ridge and look for the roving herd. But there is no roving herd to be seen. He takes them down a cut and out into the flat grasslands. Eventually, one of the hunters grows agitated and hollers out, "Where are they? I thought you people could talk to animals." Without a word, the Indian guide stands on his horse's shoulders and peers off to the horizon. They all stare at the horizon too, trying to see what he is seeing.

With all the hunters silently watching, mystified, he gets down off his horse and puts his ear to the ground and lets out a sorrowful groan.

"What? What is it?

"Buffalo come," the Indian guide says, saddened.

"Where? How do you know?" one of the hunters asks.

"Ear, wet and sticky."

Dad knows no other way to teach you the difference between people and animals, but he knows enough to teach you if you don't laugh, you'll cry.

He makes sure to point out Buffalo Bill Cody's house every time you pass, shaking a clenched fist, save his middle finger.

CITIZEN'S ARREST

"SEE WHAT THIS GUY'S DOING?" Dad says, and points toward the rearview mirror with his head and lips, hands still at ten and two.

"The car behind us?"

"Yeah, the cop."

"He's a cop?" you ask.

"Look at his headlights, they're rectangles. Two on each side of the grill. It's a Dodge Diplomat. You can see them from a mile off without even having to look at the rooftop," Dad says, wagging his pointer finger to let you know what he's doing is a no-no. "They try to creep up on motorists at night. Bunch of dumb sons of bitches."

This makes you peer into the mirror so you can see for yourself.

"He's getting too close to even see his headlights, Dad."

"It's called a speed trap."

"He's going to hurt us."

"No, he's trying to get us to break the speed limit, so he can write us a ticket. It turns into thirty miles an hour up here," he says, nodding his head down the road toward the off-ramp.

"Slow down, Dad. Please."

You know he's not listening, so you sit up straight in the seat and grab hold of the handle on the door of the Duster. He's gunning it, making the engine growl. The rumble under the hood matches the one you know is building inside Dad's chest. You've made him have that same look on his face more times than you could count.

Once the road begins to curve, and the cop's headlights disappear from the side view mirror, Dad tromps on the brake and sends his car sliding up the off-ramp.

In a blink, he throws it in neutral, sets the e-brake, flings the door open, and he's gone.

You hear yelling over the engine as it knocks to a stall. The mirror is no help, so you turn around in the seat and get up on your knees, rest your chin on the top of the headrest.

Through the swirl of red and blue lights, you watch while the deputy gets pulled from his car and tossed to the ground.

Dad slaps him.

And slaps him.

He keeps slapping him with his bare hands, the way he did with you the time at the cabin when you were trying to get away from Grandma, but when you moved the metal chair out of your way and set it back down behind you, one of the feet landed perfectly on her big toe and broke it, blackening it almost instantaneously.

He keeps slapping him with those paws of his until the deputy curls up into a ball. Dad handcuffs him and crawls into his cruiser and calls his boss to come get him.

It's a citizen's arrest, Dad says.

Dad isn't bothered by guns and badges. He reminds Mom of this on the day of their divorce. He tells her if she asks for you, he'll kill you, her, himself, right then and there in the courtroom. Before the trial began, he makes sure to tell the bailiff, "Mine's bigger than yours," eyeballing his waistline. The bailiff is young and dumb and has it in his head Dad is talking about cock size. What he's too stupid to realize is that Dad's talking about the caliber of the pistol and the length of the barrel he has tucked into his Wranglers.

Dad doesn't get custody of you on account of his history of violent behavior, according to their divorce papers. Mom gets awarded child support, but Dad stops working the very next day, and she never sees a dime. He laughs when he tells you this, says she didn't know how much money he really made until that day in court.

It takes Mom about nine months of waitressing and locksmithing and dancing before it gets too cold for you and her and Sam to sleep in the car anymore, so she calls her ex-mother-in-law and asks, "Do you want David for Christmas?"

"Of course," Grandma Audrey says. "We'd love to have him."

Mom drops you off the next day, two weeks before your birthday.

A few weeks later, Grandma Audrey tracks down Mom and asks when she'll be coming to get you, but what Grandma didn't understand is that when Mom asked if she'd like you for Christmas, she meant as a Christmas gift.

THE THINGS THAT COME OUT OF THE CLOSET

EVERYONE SAID YOU WERE LEFT on Grandma Audrey's doorstep. Everyone, meaning: Grandma Audrey and Dad. Once upon a time, you believed every word. But wasn't Oliver Twist left on a doorstep? So was Swee'Pea, right?

So why not you?

When questions are first asked concerning your mother's whereabouts, Grandma says she's dead. Debbie's mom died when she was little, which is why she went to live with Grandma. So why not say the same thing about your mother? Moms die in head-on collisions on the freeway. It's something you learn to accept as a child.

Dad won't offer an answer of his own, though you've come to conclude everything he spews stinks of bullshit. He once told a story about how when he was five a bully made him get a ball out of the street, and how he got hit by a car and how the car threw him a hundred feet through the air and how he landed in the intersection and how the ambulance got T-boned by a dump truck on the way to the hospital and how he spent the next year in a three-quarter body cast and skull cap—all to explain how he got the two scars on the front of his legs and why he didn't go to Vietnam like all of your friends' dads did. But then Grandma shows you the newspaper articles, and Dad shows you a plaster skullcap signed by his whole kindergarten class when they visited him in the hospital, and then you don't know what to believe when he opens his mouth, so it all becomes fact: The Gospel of Dick.

Something else Grandma likes to tell you is how "Arnold Schwarzenegger, Sylvester Stallone, and Dolph Lundgren, they all talk funny 'cause they're on them steroids." That's atop her saying, "Jogging is no good for you because it juggles up your insides." Now, put the aforementioned alongside how she says, "Jiggaboos are only here for our entertainment. That's why they're so good at singing and dancing and sports. That's why they're all over the damn television set." Yet when everyone sets out on the weekly pilgrimage to the Chinese restaurant after church every Sunday, you know better than to pick up the spoon, knife, and fork the waitress brings to the table. You don't even dare unfurl the napkin wrapped around them. Eating by any other means than chopsticks means a trip to the parking lot. You will not disrespect their culture.

But if all of this is confusing, it is nowhere as complicated as the first time you see a Black lady at the mall. When you ask her if she is a *Goddamned Jew*, she knows to not get mad at you. Instead, she scans the crowd of shoppers and asks one or two of the women, "Does this little boy belong to you?" but no one answers her, so you're left to wander and weave through the maze of clothing racks back to Grandma without further incident.

Grandma Audrey's parenting skills aren't rinse, lather, repeat. With your dad, it was one favor after another. Nowadays, if anyone asks her for a favor, she fires back with, "Who was your slave last year?"

To make a long story short: she never did you any favors. Well, maybe one, depending on how loosely you define favor. Washing one's mouth out with soap doesn't sound so bad, though *washing* makes it seem like it's followed by being rinsed out, the way it happens at the dentist's office, when your mouth is left feeling refreshed and minty. Grandma Audrey makes sure you swallow every last drop. Nothing went wasted in her house.

Liquid Palmolive is tough on grease and soft on hands, but it also gives you the screaming shits for days on end.

She pinches off your air, yanks your nose up toward the ceiling, slaps her other hand over your lips, tilts your head back so far you slide up onto your tippy-toes—you can't fight this part, it's simple mechanics. You can't breathe, not that she cares, she is waiting for the reflex to kick in and your body to gulp down the dish detergent as if it was air. This is how drowning victims' lungs fill with water. When you fight it, she says, "I'll rip your nose right off your face." To stop yourself from falling, you moonwalk. She tells you to stop fighting her, stop trying to get away, but you're only trying to stop from falling over. God help you if you choke while gasping for a breath and spit any of it out onto the floor or onto her blouse. She slipped once, almost head-butting you, knocking her glasses off her face and down onto the floor. Luckily for her, she let go and clawed down your face and neck with her fingernails, breaking her fall. It's as if she expects you to swallow it down like a teaspoon of bubblegum-flavored cough syrup. But even when it comes to that, she can make something so sweet so sour.

For calling a girl a slut in the sixth grade, the punishment is two mouthfuls of soap. You're a head taller by then, so she drags a chair out into the center of the kitchen floor and makes you sit. And this may sound like you came home from school and strolled out into the kitchen and took a seat after setting down your bookbag. But that's not how this took place.

She watches for you out the window and hauls you by the hair into the kitchen, bent at the waist yet simultaneously teetering on your tippy-toes every step of the way. You know not to fight her, though you could. Her kitchen is an armory full of wooden spoons, metal spatulas, metal fly swatters, metal-edged yardsticks, and a marble rolling pin—all of which she can, has, and will readily wield well outside the manufacturer's intended purpose. History tells you teachers won't or don't ever ask what happened. They don't even care at Sunday school.

Swallowing mouthfuls of soap is not something the body wants to do, even if the mind says to go along with it and get it over with as quickly as possible—kind of like when you try to put in eye drops. These sorts of protests are automatic, like when you slam your mouth shut and snap your head from side to side when she brings the bottle to your lips—or any other time someone tries to force something inside of you.

This is called a segue, one which leads back to that girl—the so-called slut. She had three abortions before she began high school. At twelve, she got knocked up by her big brother's friend, and later, who knows who else. But she isn't a slut. She was raped. She didn't call it that, but that is what happens when a high schooler has sex with a girl in grade school.

When Dad hears what you said to the girl, Debbie lets him know you've already been disciplined, that he doesn't need to do anything, that she and Grandma already took care of it, that you got dish soap and screamed at and grounded for a week. But double jeopardy doesn't exist in his eyes.

He doesn't holler out your name and wait for you to come downstairs so he can give you a talking to. Rather, he clomps up the flight of stairs, takes hold of your ankle, pulls you from the top bunk, and lets gravity do the rest. Before you can catch a breath, he grabs you by the neck and slams you against the wall until your hair sticks into the wood paneling and piss splashes on his boots.

How dare you?

He's infuriated, so he slams you harder, telling you to "Stop pissing all over the damn place, sissy." You do as you're told. Instead, blood drips down the leg of your pants and onto his snakeskin boots as this latest concussion lulls you to sleep.

The good thing about being beaten until you lose consciousness is how you don't remember the grisly parts, the parts where you've stopped trying to protect yourself and instead give in to being tossed around like Debbie's Raggedy Ann doll, the parts where your head and face and guts and nuts get kneaded like dough. This one is a memory that haunts your sister, not you, and that's another segue.

The first time you have sex, it's in an abandoned barn. He's holding you down. He's twice your size, twice your age, too. Your face is buried in his chest. You can't see, but you can smell. Maybe that's why you remember this so viscerally?

His musk mixes with the smell of spoiled, forgotten hay, cushioning your back from the floorboards of an abandoned barn's hayloft. It quiets his grunts and groans and the guttural sounds you'll never shake, the sounds that will never stop sending shivers across your skin. His sweat mats the hair on his chest, and that hair drags across your face, chest, shoulders. His sweat stings and sets your eyes on fire.

You turn away, turn toward the door where the bales are hoisted up into the barn, toward the outside, toward the perfect blue cloudless sky.

The afternoon sun becomes blinding, but not bright enough for the outside world to see what is happening. What is happening? You don't possess the words to describe it. Not yet. Don't talk. Stay quiet. Don't get hurt. Get outside yourself. What is he doing? is a question that keeps swirling around in the back of your brain, draining down into whatever recesses days like this go to hide. How did he get you there? Somehow, *that's* the part you've blocked out.

When his weight lifts off you, your privates and belly are wet, warm, sticky, stinking. What he left behind pools in your belly button. He rises to his knees, leaving you covered in his sweat and shadow. He warns you he could flip you over and give you AIDS. You don't know what it means. Only that it's bad. So bad you remember hearing how Aunt Bobbie's brother-in-law got it and jumped off the Bong Bridge to die less painlessly.

Before you say one thing, he looks down and says, "See? You liked it," and reminds you of how you could've stayed at Grandma Audrey's cabin.

But he actually invited you away from the cabin, away from Grandma. He rescued you from her for an afternoon. "Remember that," he says.

The two of you go for a swim as soon as you get back to the cabin—to wash off the mess. The evidence.

You don't tell Grandma.

"If you do, none of the other big cousins will invite you to come with when they go for walks again. They'll leave you there with Audrey," he says, right before the two of you walk up the steps of the screened-in front porch.

All of the cousins thought he was weird. He never wanted to play Cowboys and Indians or Cops and Robbers or Army Men. Instead, he asked to play Charlie's Angels, but he didn't want to be Charlie, and the only girl at the cabin then was Debbie. But what makes any of that worth remembering? Who knows? Who cares? You work to forget him. He isn't even a real cousin. He's a removed cousin. Or a second cousin. He's Dad's cousin's kid—whatever you call that. He isn't two-spirit, either. He has no soul.

It must have been the summer before the sixth grade, or maybe the fifth. It's not like you can keep track of all the times he took you for walks. But by the end of the sixth grade, you find that giant dishtowel Grandma made to drape over the kitchen table waving in the wind on the clothesline. It's still wet, so it takes some work, but eventually looks like a noose from *Gunsmoke* and the history specials on PBS when they punished bank robbers and Black folks who ran away.

The neighbor lady paid somebody to trim the bottom boughs from her trees, so you have to take a lawn chair with you to get up there.

The noose goes on like a backward necktie after the other end is knotted to a branch thick as your thigh. The lawn chair has to be kicked away. Even that doesn't come easy for you, meaning: it scoots a time or two before it folds and falls away from your feet.

Your face burns and your body spins when the towel untangles. The water wrings out and drips down your back while your vision blurs the green siding of Grandma's house into the canary yellow of the Millers' and the institutional white of the duplex where you're dangling—fast at first, then things slow. One silhouette morphs into the next. The different houses lose their individual shapes and become a kaleidoscope. Then the towel tears, and you plop down onto the ground. You land with a root right in between your shoulder blades. The air vacates your lungs, which inflate with pain and fear you've never known. All you can do is watch what's left of the white dishtowel wave in the wind. Next to your hand lies the button that popped off the husky jeans Grandma bought for you the week before. You want to leave her home, but you're too fat to do even that.

BACK TO BASICS

REMEMBER BOOT CAMP? YEAH, MAYBE you've worked to forget everything about the time you spent in uniform, but things just keep bubbling back up. Basic in Benning is one of those things.

There was the matter of the nervous shits on the plane ride south. The first time you ever rode on one.

Your first set of push-ups followed you asking one of the drill sergeants if you could switch to a bottom bunk because you sleep like a cement truck and were sure to fall sometime during the night.

His response was, "Drop, push-ups, go."

He was a reception drill sergeant, so he didn't get all fancy with his verbiage, meaning: he did not order you to assume the front-leaning rest position. But you still got his meaning. About an hour after the lights went out, he realized you weren't exaggerating about the cement truck thing when he heard you slap against the concrete floor after a six-foot fall. "For fuck's sake, son" was his response. "You hit the floor so hard it woke me up inside the office." It woke you up, too, is what you tell him. That right there should have signaled your capacity for sarcasm in the face of pain, but they didn't quite catch on. They will, eventually. But they'll smoke you innumerable times beforehand.

The first time they told you, "You're about to get smoked, Private. Do you want to get smoked?" you said you were not sure, you didn't know what it was. They informed you—all of you—that smoking is when they exercise you so intensely steam rises from your body. One particular private earned the nickname of Smokey. Not you. You get christened Frosty, like the snowman, because you never stop sweating once, like a snowman in the summertime. You shed twenty-seven pounds in fourteen weeks. But let's not get ahead of ourselves.

Smokey ended up going to a different company than you, so the last smoke session you saw starring him ended with a reception battalion drill sergeant asking him, "How do you like me now?" to which Smokey replied, "Drill Sergeant, who told you I liked you in the first place, Drill Sergeant?" Luckily for Smokey, two other drill sergeants pulled the first drill sergeant away. It probably wouldn't have been so infuriating had several hundred privates who were supposed to be silently staring at the back of the head of the private in front of them not suddenly erupted in laughter.

The real drill sergeants tore through records looking for gang members, juvie records, anyone with a history of violence—morality waivers, as the Army sometimes calls them—while the unsuspecting privates all sat on benches and ate bagged meals and begged to use the bathroom. Sorry. Latrine. Begged because the drill sergeants could finish up at any moment, signaling the official start of boot camp. They are looking for the crème de la crap, not the poster boys and boy scouts you see on the commercials.

Those who make the cut are loaded onto literal livestock trailers and sent to a training battalion nicknamed the House of Pain. What follows the truck reaching its destination is known as the shark attack. In the movies, this is depicted with a bunch of privates pouring off a bus and lining up into a perfect formation, circled by screaming drill sergeants—a few tears stream down cheeks, etc.

That's not how they do it at the House of Pain.

When the tractor-trailers pull up, those who can peer out the holes tell the rest of you how it's just one guy waiting. A lot of pomp and circumstance. "Stressing us for no good reason," someone says.

This one guy is the single biggest man you've ever come across in real life. With a drill sergeant's Smokey Bear hat perched atop his head, he is every bit of seven feet tall.

The first few privates ooze out the narrow doors with their duffle bags strapped to their backs, and he says nothing. He doesn't even seem to blink. He could be a mannequin. Seconds ticked by as privates grunt and groan their way out of the cattle hauler and look to him for guidance, of which he offers none until he is surrounded with stupefied privates. That's when he raises his monstrous hands into the sky and screams, "Move, you fucking retards!" and brings his hands back down and slaps the duffle bags strapped to their backs, pushing them forward.

Again, he shouts, "Move!" and points to the far end of the building, where another drill sergeant waits, one so small you're sure there's a pygmy somewhere in his lineage. Somewhere recent. His father. Possibly his grandfather. He is the goal post, and you haul ass down to him. He says nothing, only points toward the company area. That's where the sharks are circling. Seeing this, some privates freeze, trying to make out what all is being said by the dozen or so drill sergeants who are waiting on three platoons' worth of privates and think it adds to the atmosphere if they all talk at the same time.

The herd of privates forms a bottleneck of sorts, one that the big bastard takes full advantage of when he walks up behind them and begins shoving duffle bags. Some privates topple to the ground. Others smash into other privates who then domino other privates into the walls. The privates who fall are made to push Georgia while they are down there. The rest make a mad dash to the platoon areas. Any platoon areas. No one goes where they are supposed to. That isn't how this works. There's a lot of name-calling; last name, first name, you stand here—that kind of thing. Not schoolyard name-calling. That comes later. Once you are put in your proper place, you're told to situate your duffle bag between your feet and take a seat and hold your ID card in one hand and your dog tags in the other, as high in the air as you can, and stare straight ahead while awaiting further instructions.

All this goes on while the drill sergeants are doing everything they can to confuse you and talk over one another. No good can come of this. Luckily, you find your place in time to see some private scramble to the platoon area where he's been summoned by his drill sergeant, only to be stopped midway and dropped for push-ups by a different drill sergeant.

There is a prescribed way to do everything. Push-ups especially. Both hands meet the ground simultaneously, shoulder-width apart, fingers spread, thumbs pointed toward each other. Feet are kicked all the way back, and you are to make your entire body—head, spine, buttocks, legs—into a straight line. This is the framed front-leaning rest position.

When that private kicks out his feet, he does so with such force and such terrible timing that he takes the company commander's legs out from underneath him and sends him somersaulting.

Someone hits the mute button.

Not a sound is heard in the company area until the captain rises to his feet, brushes himself off, politely asks the private, "What is your name, young man," and says something to the drill sergeant, who then informs the private who he's just kicked—assaulted, technically—and that he's already looking at an Article 15—disciplinary action.

Upstairs, things don't calm down any. The platoon files in, taking up positions beside beds that line the outside walls and wrap around the interior in alphabetical order. Each bed is numbered. Your number is zero-four-nine. Once the drill sergeants are certain no missteps were made with the alphabetization, they call the platoon forward to await further instructions, which requires the platoon to gather around the teeny-tiny drill sergeant outside the office door.

Someone silently farts, an action this drill sergeant takes personally. He doesn't drop the platoon as a group or attempt to suss out the offending individual or even ask for the culprit to reveal themselves. In fact, he only belts out, "Drink water," in the singsong sort of way the Army teaches you, to which the privates holler back, in unison, "Beat the heat, Drill Sergeant, beat the heat."

"Both canteens, gentlemen," he says. "This is Georgia. It is August. Stay hydrated. Drink water." He sings those two simple words beautifully.

To illustrate both canteens have been emptied into your gullet, they are held overhead with the caps unscrewed. When everyone finishes, he says, "Go fill them back up, gentlemen. Form back up right here on me," and the platoon sprints into the latrine at the opposite end of the barracks and does as ordered as fast as possible.

Once every canteen is full, and every private has formed back up, the drill sergeant belts out, "Drink water," in his soulful Sunday choir best. And you all do as you're told.

Both canteens, again.

Someone pukes. Judging by the unbroken cadence of his monologue, the drill sergeant does not acknowledge the sound of the retching nor the splashing water spilling down onto his freshly waxed floor. More privates puke. He does not mention it or voice his concern. Instead, he patiently waits while emptied canteens are displayed overhead, two by two. After which, he orders them filled up again. And drunk, again.

This goes on for five trips to the latrine. It goes on until every private sips their water and immediately pukes that same water down onto their boots.

Most double-time to the latrine to vomit, at first, too proud to puke on the floor, or afraid of the unknown punishment for doing so. You've never known love until you've shared a toilet bowl with another person and effectively held onto one another to stop from faceplanting into the water while violently retching.

This is how you make the acquaintance of one Cesar Barraza. You will always roll your tongue when you say his name. That's not to say you always see eye to eye with him.

One morning he walks up to the sink where you're shaving and begins to brush his teeth. You blink a handful of times after catching sight of his eyebrow in the mirror, blackened and swollen and stitched shut. Naturally, you ask, "What happened?"

"Shut the fuck up, Frosty," he growls back through a mouthful of frothing toothpaste.

While tightening up your bunk, you ask the guy who sleeps across from you if he knows what happened to Barraza. He laughs, asks you how your hand feels.

"Last night," he says, "when he went to wake you for fire watch, you stood up, still asleep. Sleepwalking, right? And you hauled off and cold-cocked him upside the head and laid him right out on the floor. Then you lay back down like it was part of a dream."

"What?"

"Ask Trimble if you don't believe me. Drill sergeant came through and took him to the ER. Watch rotation was all fucked up."

"Fuck!"

"Fuck is right. Trimble took your watch."

"What? Why?"

"Hey, Trimble," he says, "why didn't you wake Tromblay up for watch?"

"'Cause fuck getting knocked out is why."

That's not the only problem you had sleeping while at the Infantry Training Battalion. Problem is kind of an odd term to use here, really. You'd wake whenever a mouse let a fart go and fall back to sleep just as quick.

Once you heard one of the fire watches announce to the other private the presence of a drill sergeant in the barracks by hissing, "Stand by." It seems you heard those two whispered words over all the snoring and farting and tossing and turning and whatever was going on inside your very own dream and hopped out of bed and stood at the end of your bunk—and fell right back asleep where you stood.

"Private," the drill sergeant said in your ear, waking you.

"Yes, Drill Sergeant?" you said.

"Carry on."

"Yes, Drill Sergeant," you said, looking around and realizing he wanted you to crawl back into your bunk.

The next morning, while everyone was preparing for the day, you heard him say to himself and whoever might be listening, "Some privates sleepwalk, but this motherfucker does drill and ceremony in his sleep. Hell, he might even be the Manchurian Candidate."

Privates learned to sleep anywhere. In line waiting on a truck was the best sleep you could get. An entire platoon would stand shoulder to shoulder, lined up by squad. Unless you were in the front row, all you had to do was rest your chin on top of the bedroll atop the next private's rucksack and close your eyes. The one time you found yourself up front, you got creative. You fixed the bayonet onto your M16 and placed its buttstock on the ground. Next, all you had to do was spin the bayonet's sheath upside down on your utility belt, slide it back in, and, bingo, you'd made yourself into a tripod. Lights out.

Out on the soft sawdust of the PT field, you are taught proper stretching and exercise techniques, and how much water you need to take in while sweating under the Georgia summer sun. The lot of you are some fifty feet from the field latrine, which is basically a concrete cube with a trough along one wall and a half a dozen toilets lining the other, sans privacy stalls.

But there's no need to worry about using either at this point.

Every single private who asks the drill sergeant leading the demonstration whether they can utilize the latrine is denied. Every time someone does ask, he tells them to drink more water, putting more pressure on their bladders. By the third time he tells the platoon to drink water, he hears an unmistakable sound and loses all semblance of professionalism. He zigzags through the formation, demanding to know who's pouring their water out onto the field. "Speak up now," he says. He'll smoke the shit out of the platoon, he threatens—until he comes upon Alphabet pissing himself.

Alphabet is so named because the combination of his first, last, and middle names lacks only two letters from the alphabet. That, and not a single one of the drill sergeants can pronounce it. You're able to pronounce it. He's in the same part of the alphabet as you, so he sleeps one bed away. Like you, he's spent most of his life since puberty studying the martial arts. When the drill sergeants get wind of this, they put the two of you against one another during hand-to-hand combat training one day. It hardly seems worth mentioning, other than the fact that they also place money on the two of you.

The second week is the week you learn basic first aid. The day of the practicals is an all-day affair. Once you pass one of the stations, you go back to sit with your platoon, where you will stay until you all pass and you are all ordered on to the next station, unless you have to use the latrine. If you have to shit, you use the latrine. If you have to piss, you use the woodline, meaning: you run off somewhere inside the trees and piss. Which you do. By this point, it's already been instilled in you to wait until the last minute to go, so it is a *long* piss, but not so long that you notice how you're standing next to a trail that leads to another first aid training station.

Mid-piss, you see the company commander coming your way. At first, you look away, pretend you don't see him, hope you can finish up and take off before he gets so close you have to render a salute. But you're taking a piss, so, are you supposed to salute? What did they teach you? Literally drill into you? When in doubt, salute.

So you do.

You put your heels together, let go of your dick with your right hand, and offer the captain a crisp salute and say, "Good afternoon, sir." It's a salute he does not return. Instead, he tells you, "Two hands, Private, two hands," and walks right by you. The rest of the day, the drill sergeants just laugh when they see you.

The next time you have a one-on-one with the company commander follows a weekend bivouac. It's lunchtime back at battalion headquarters. A weekend-long bivouac means it's been three days since you've eaten actual food. And it's been three days since you shit, too. MRE, for you, means Meal Refuses to Exit.

But midway through your lunch, you realize those nine or ten MREs have all changed their mind and are ready to exit. That means you have to devour what's left on your tray, drink your remaining water, put the tray and your glasses on the conveyor belt so they can go back into the kitchen, leave the chow hall, hop up on the pull-up bars, knock out ten pull-ups, then double-time it back to the company area, then scale three flights of stairs, then find an open stall in your platoon's latrine.

As you're trotting with ass cheeks clenched, the company commander comes around the corner. Seeing this, you let go of an audible "Fuck," because you know you have to slow to a walk and render the captain a salute and wait for him to return your salute before you can continue on your way. But there is no way, not today. Instead, you pretend you didn't see him. You kick up the pace to a full sprint.

"Private!" he says. "Where are you going?"

You look back to see it's you he's addressing, being it's only the two of you in the breezeway. He's at a standstill, still looking in the direction he was walking when you ran by him. You *have* to go back.

You face him and salute him and say, "Good afternoon, sir," while your butthole begins to quiver.

"Where are you headed, Private?"

"To the latrine, sir."

"And you couldn't take the time to render a proper salute?"

"I need the latrine, sir."

"How many seconds does it take to salu—"

He can't finish his sentence because you can't hold your shit any longer. He goes completely silent. It's just him and you standing there with a weekend's worth of digested MREs exploded inside your uniform trousers.

His expression tells you to carry on; he doesn't have to say it. He's already walking away. But you still render a parting salute and offer him a "Mountaineers, sir."

You come to realize boot camp is more like a slice of America's prison population. The drill sergeants point out, "In times of financial downfall, more white guys are coming through these barracks. We have a few more than usual right now, which says it would be a bad time to leave the Army because the job market sucks. The exception is the white trash. We see a lot of those. And even with your shaved head and uniform, we can still pick you out of a crowd."

Another drill sergeant chimes in, "Watch. You, you scrawny little shit, the one who looks like he's wearing his daddy's uniform, where are you from?"

"Shenandoah, West Virginia, Drill Sergeant."

"Shedding Dog, West Virginia? I fucking knew it. A no-shit hillbilly."

"Shan-in-dough-ah, Drill Sergeant."

"Got a question, Private. You ever seen a black person before coming here?"

"Nah, Drill Sergeant."

"Nah?"

"No, Drill Sergeant. Sorry, Drill Sergeant."

"Now you think I'm a sorry drill sergeant. Is that right?"

"Naw—ah—"

"Stop stuttering, Private. Who's your battle buddy?"

"Roster number zero-two-four, Drill Sergeant."

"Not unless it's that big Shaft-looking motherfucker in the back corner, it ain't—Private, where are you from? Please say Chicago or Compton or some shit."

"Arkansas, Drill Sergeant."

"Shit, you're a hillbilly too, ain't ya, Private?"

"Yes, Drill Sergeant," he says. Both he and his new battle buddy hang their heads a little.

That's how it works. The platoon drill sergeant, like a warden and his guards, make life so miserable that you don't have it in you anymore to worry about your differences. You're bonded by the shittiness of it all.

Still, sixty or so men trapped in one room, no matter how large, never proves large enough. The expression rats in a cage is a tried and true metaphor.

When one private sucker punches another private, the three platoons sit and watch their first Article 15 proceedings. An Article 15 is a hearing for non-judicial punishment where an officer immediately above the offending individual or individuals is either awarded a punishment, such as extra duty, or it can be deemed that a Courts Martial hearing is more appropriate.

When all is said and done, the two privates are given extra duties for the following month. Not a big deal. One was in trouble for throwing the punch, the other for instigating the assault.

Now, as with most military goings-on, a debriefing followed. That's where your supervisor breaks down the thing you just saw or did, so everyone understands what happened. The two privates involved in the Article 15 debacle weren't from your platoon. They were from second. So your platoon sergeant gathered all of the third platoon outside his office and launched into a monologue you'll never forget.

"Men, are there any squabbles inside this platoon we need to squash? I have duty tonight, and I will check out the pugil gear, and we can do it right here. It'll be done with. Speak up!—fine. I have been in a few fights during my time in the Army. I've served with more than a few dickheads who needed their attitude adjusted. And I was happy to oblige. Call it a calling."

"Hooah."

"Now, what I didn't do was walk up to the guy in full goddamn uniform with my name sewn on my shirt and punch that motherfucker in the teeth. Gentlemen, the Army has issued you so many things. One is a ski mask. That's what you wear. Just that. Only that. Boots, too. Sorry, I forgot boots. Now, you put on your ski mask and your boots, and you wait until you know that motherfucker will be in the latrine alone. Then you beat his ass. What, you think any self-respecting soldier is going to report an assault and say, *Yes, sir, there I was on my way into the latrine after PT and this guy assaulted me. Well, what did he look like? He was naked, sir. Naked? You didn't recognize his face? He had on a ski mask, sir. Any identifying marks? I didn't look closely at him, but his dick did hang down to his knees, sir.* No! They ain't going to say shit. They'll tell the doc they tripped or some shit, but no one will ever report being beaten up by a naked man. Though if you're covered in tattoos like some of you dumbfucks, I can't help you. Understand what I'm telling you, men?"

"Hooah!"

Turns out he wasn't lying. About a week and a half later, someone from the first platoon decided they had a beef with someone from the third platoon, and they were going to risk some extra duty and jump him first chance they got. And word spread. And maybe the third platoon and first platoon wanted it to happen. But the first platoon didn't know what third had in mind.

One night, things came to a boiling point in the laundry room. The guy from third platoon retreated back to the barracks, and the guy from first platoon was held back by a few of his more level-headed battle buddies. But eventually, he crept his way into third platoon's barracks and found his sworn enemy sitting on the floor quietly polishing a pair of boots. The lack of boots by the bunks gave him the extra push to bum-rush the guy. By his best guess, half of the platoon was downstairs washing clothes, others were out on the PT field, and the rest were nowhere close enough to worry him.

When the pair of latrine doors swung open and out poured a platoon of men wearing nothing more than boots and ski masks, who cut off his escape route and bum-rushed him as well, he forgot all that ever angered him. The third platoon never even spoke a word. The soft clomp of the hundred-plus rubber soles making their way toward him was enough to make him cower. The sight of sixty or so swinging dicks was enough to get him begging to leave. And that may be why first and second platoon stopped using third platoon's moniker and motto: *Mountaineers, climb to glory!* and instead started saying *Mountainqueers, climb your buddy!* while getting away from us as fast as possible.

The House of Pain had a storied past—rumors of investigations, acts which led to a handful of drill sergeants losing their hats. A cycle before you showed up, a private completed a run and began to complain that his chest hurt. The drill sergeant ordered him to stand at attention when addressing him, so the private did as told. He stood erect, heels together, feet at a forty-five-degree angle, slight bend at the knee, arms at his side, hands along the seam of his shorts, head and eyes looking straight forward.

Once he'd assumed the proper position, the drill sergeant asked him what his problem was. Again, he told the drill sergeant his chest was hurting. In response, the drill sergeant planted his foot in the private's sternum and asked, "How about now?" laughing while the private bounced off the wall behind him and collapsed. By best guess, he was dead before he hit the ground. That's why they aren't filming for the boot camp video all the other battalions get.

But the drill sergeants don't scare you. There are rules of what they can and cannot do. If they break those rules, they'll lose their hat and maybe even their careers. You know you're safe with them.

The monster of a drill sergeant, the one-man welcoming committee, catches on after a while, whispers to you once while you're cleaning your weapon: "I know you come from a real fucked-up home. You're not afraid of us. We don't want you to be afraid of us. We want to teach you all we can, so you can live as long as you can out on the battlefield. You got it? How about you calm down some and let us do our job? You're not at home anymore. You got out. You survived all that shit."

You stay quiet, don't even look up at him. You don't want him to see your eyes well.

Four years later, you find yourself in North Chicago in the pipeline to become a Sailor, which you do with ease.

TRICK OR TREAT

"What the hell is that noise?"
"Falling
    Down
        The stairs,
            What's
                It
                    Sound
                        Like?"

It's a miracle you don't break a rib, or Grandma doesn't bust a yardstick across your butt for making a smart-aleck comment while tumbling down the stairs. No one bothers to get out of their seat or come see what's going on, but Grandpa Bub does lean forward to peer into the darkness of the front hallway in time to watch you finish falling down the last few stairs. The Yoda costume, which isn't really much more than a thick trash bag with his brown robe printed on it, works a whole lot like a Slip 'N Slide when the slack gets caught underfoot.

You don't crush the plastic mask. Thankfully, it's waiting on the kitchen table along with a pillowcase.

Grandpa Bub nods to Grandma Audrey, affirming you are indeed falling down the stairs, and you are, in fact, narrating what is happening while it is happening. You don't dare ignore her. You know enough to answer her when she asks a question.

Her face is one of bewilderment. Not that you paid any attention, but it's always the main plot point whenever the story is rehashed by Debbie. It's perplexing how she isn't chasing you around the house for saying what you said, and you don't want to push your luck, so you grab the mask and pillowcase and head out the door with your big cousin, Glen, who already has a hold of the doorknob.

The two of you fill your pillowcases three times total, and Dad steals everything made of solid chocolate, claiming it's for warmth when he's out in the deer stand.

You cover every street in the surrounding square mile. It's simple: you two go to the houses with their front porch lights turned on and ignore the darkened ones.

When the two of you take note of a house that is decorated as can be but not lit by a single bulb, you get curious. The door is propped open, and there are fake cobwebs everywhere, with giant plastic spiders dangling down from the ceiling of the front porch. Ominous laughter loops from a little speaker mounted next to some pumpkins that have burned out.

You knock.

Nothing.

You ring the doorbell.

Nothing.

Glen says, "David," nudging your elbow, "scarecrow."

At the opposite end of the porch is a scarecrow slumped on a bench. Between its feet is a Tupperware bowl full of candy. The good stuff. Pinned to its chest is a sign reading: *take one.*

There's two of you, so you take two and put one in Glen's pillowcase. When you turn to leave, Glen shakes his head and says, "Uh-uh, don't be a pussy," quiet enough so whoever is inside the house won't hear him. That's followed by "Grab a handful," which you do. Then you hear Glen say, "Oh shit!" loud enough for everyone to hear.

That's when someone takes hold of your wrist and growls, "I said one!"

The scarecrow stands over you, laughing, clenching the wrist attached to the greedy hand that plunged into the candy bowl one time too many. Your "Lemme go" is more of a sound, somewhere between a moan and a whimper.

The scarecrow growls, "Can't you read?" and the arm continues to tug and yank away from him like a headless flopping fish. But he's got to be six foot tall and two hundred pounds with no way out of his grip.

Still, Yoda does all he can to turn and run.

There's nervous sweat pouring beneath that costume. That wrist slips from the scarecrow's grip, and Yoda makes it out the front porch door. Though, there's the matter of a few stairs which have somehow slipped the mind. Yoda slams down to the ground, the costume splits up the side, and you spill out.

Glen is gone.

The only sign of him is the fading frantic sound of his footfalls traveling farther away. The scarecrow stands atop the front porch stairs, flings the pillowcase, and says, "Don't forget your candy," laughing himself into a stupor.

Over on the next block, you find Glen standing beneath a streetlight laughing, saying, "Holy shit," over and over again. "Grandma's going to kill you," lifting a torn flap of vinyl costume that was once Master Yoda's robe.

CLEANING OUT THE CLOSET

WHILE CLEANING UP THE FRONT hallway after the holidays, Grandma gives you a handful of coat hangers and tells you to put them away. They're the old wire kind, the ones she gets from the dry cleaners. You don't want her to tell you again, but she's standing right in front of the closet door, taking drags off her cigarette, contemplating what chore she'll have you tackle next. You know if you say "Excuse me," she'll say "I'll move when I'm goddamn good and ready," so you do that clumsy dance of left then right then left again while she shakes her head ever so slightly, causing you to suspect she might have early-stage Parkinson's, until she lifts her eyebrows from back behind her bifocals, signaling her patience has run out. This is the look that accompanies her saying, "Hurry the hell up." But there's no telling whether she said it this time or if she even needs to say it anymore. It's Pavlovian at this point.

She blows a billow of smoke and looks down at you with a bored glare. Through the smoke, you mumble, "You're closer," and almost hand the hangers to her before it dawns on you what you've said aloud.

She snatches the coat hangers away from you and coils her hand up over her head, wafting away the halo of smoke clinging to her curlers. You fall to the floor—the way the fainting goats do when you bum rush them at the petting zoo—covering yourself the best you can, pinning your chin to your chest, cupping your hands over your ears, making yourself the smallest possible target. It's the same as what the sergeants teach you during boot camp in preparation for a nuclear attack, but by the time they get a hold of you, it's instinct for you to curl up in a ball and kiss your ass goodbye.

The sting of a wire coat hanger is nothing new. But *sting* is just a word—a placeholder, really—for the sensation that follows the lashes. There isn't a word for the feeling that comes over you while it is happening. It's confusing. It is something you feel only when it comes as a surprise, when you can't tell if it's a searing burn or a cold so deep it'll blacken flesh.

Regardless of how long it went on, it went on long enough for welts to rise on both sides of the neck, long enough for her scolding to become a scream and an incomprehensible slurry of vowels and consonants, long enough for you to no longer recognize the individual lashes—only a constant ache, akin to the time she says not to touch the toaster and when you ask her, "Why?" she plops your forearm across the top of it and presses down until you can't breathe enough to cry and then your shoes slide out from underneath you when the puddle of piss around your feet makes the linoleum too slippery to stand. You'll wear long-sleeved shirts and bandages for the next two weeks.

She tosses the hangers to the floor and snatches a handful of hair with her talons, and you exclaim a redundant reminder of what she is doing, hoping it will somehow make her stop, or, by some miracle cause someone to come to the rescue just this once.

You wait for her to say it: "I'm not pulling your hair, I'm only holding your hair. You're the one hopping around like a damn fool."

It's as adult as the back and forth between Debbie and you:

"Stop touching me."

"I'm not touching you."

Today she mutters through clenched teeth while pinching her cigarette between her lips, but those words escape you. All you can only hear is the blood rushing in your ears.

She tries the doorknob with her other hand, but the spring in the latch is as old as anything in the house, so it takes two or three times to get it all to catch just right, and you make it all that much worse by slumping back down to the floor while gravity, not Grandma, pulls strands of hair free from your scalp.

On the fourth or fifth try, the closet door does swing open, and she shoves you inside, where you are to stay until the next morning, you got it?

The bile-green shag carpet covering the floor of the front hallway shuts out the light cast by the brass chandelier. The closet becomes something of a cave filled with the musk of everyone's raincoats and winter parkas and your snowmobile suit, which is still damp from last night's trek to the hill behind the hair salon where Grandma goes on the mornings when Grandpa's pension check comes to the mailbox. The house falls silent, save the jingling of the coat hangers each time you shift from your left side to the right, along with the sound of Scrappy's sniffing, his checking to see if everything is all right. But he only sniffs. He doesn't paw at the door or claw at the carpet. He too is afraid to help. He too is a bystander in all this.

Not even sleep comes to the rescue that night. Not because you cower in fear, waiting for the closet door to fly open and the beating to recommence. That never crosses your mind. Getting locked away in the closet for the night is old hat. No, you don't sleep simply because you're wise enough to savor the solitude.

Somehow you never become claustrophobic. It should have made you afraid of dark, closed spaces, elevators, windowless rooms, even the turtleneck you'd have to wear to school the next day. But it doesn't. Being locked in the closet means not having to duck each time she raises a hand. It means not having to dodge a cigarette lighter each time you dare walk in front of the television set, yet you can't walk through the kitchen because she'll curse you out, thinking you're going for a glass of water when she just did the damn dishes. It means not being threatened with an obscenely early bedtime if ever you speak a word—even if it is during a commercial break. It means not having to clip her toenails or scrape out the yellow, crusty stuff collected underneath them. It means not having to drag a pumice stone across her hooves and then get kicked when you knock the dead skin off your pajama pants and onto the floor she just vacuumed. It means not having to carve her calluses off with a paring knife or moisturize her corns or rub her arches with your hands, which are never strong enough to please her and bring her the ease she needs following her long day at the job you never see her leave for—all this for the crime of being seen *and* heard.

The blackness and the quiet of the closet do not serve as a conduit for the earlier events of that afternoon to creep back into the forefront of your mind. You don't sit wondering what you should have said or done differently. Instead, that night, a scene from the cabin calls to mind.

The hum of a needle gliding across the grooves of a vinyl LP ushers in a symphony of strings, accompanied by some soft, muffled horns, the strike of a hi-hat—punctuated by the clink that comes from Grandma's glass when she swishes her brandy and 7Up while singing along with Doris Day between taking a drag off of her Raleigh Lights. All this echoes in your ears while you sit cross-legged on the closet floor, but it's so sonorous you may as well be back on the cabin's kitchen floor peering over the arm of the rocking chair, taking in the wonder of this woman at peace. Grandma's voice is velvet. It gets lost in the lyrics of "Sentimental Journey." A story of a woman who wishes to take a train and roam back home. But the mushroom cloud of cigarette smoke collecting over the coffee table does little to conceal how the man in black can make her voice quake by simply telling her a story about a Pima Indian with whom she shares a last name.

She sobs while he sings about the whiskey-drinking Indian, a Marine who went off to war, and how he died drunk in a ditch in two inches of water. He sings about the white men who stole their water rights and how the sparkling water stopped. Her grandson was born where the water stops—in Anishinaabemowin, that is: Nah-Gah-Chi-Wa-Nong. Not that she can speak a word of the language. Not that she lets on.

ALL DOGS GO TO HEAVEN

BRUTUS IS YOUR FIRST DOG, despite his not being a dog. He is a wolf. He's not a wolf-dog or a wolf hybrid, but a timber wolf, also known as the gray wolf, also known as a western wolf. Your first dog, Brutus, is a no-shit wolf. But you don't really remember him. There are a few flashes of his fur, flits of memories, and a handful of pictures faded from forty years. Brutus's pups you do remember, but not him—at least, not while the two of you lived under the same roof. You do, however, remember him at the zoo, after Dad got rid of him. The rest of Brutus's stories are told to you, not by you, so they're not really your stories to tell.

Then came Fifi, or so you're told. He was a Pekinese that belonged to Grandpa Bullshit before he died. Fifi was a birthday present, in a roundabout way, seeing as how Grandpa Bullshit died the morning you turned two. To you, *Fifi* is a word for *dog*, so when Fifi dies, Mom takes you to the pound to pick out another Fifi.

The way she tells it, you toddled from kennel to kennel until you called to get her attention, saying, "That my Cici." You can't pronounce, Fifi, but Mom knows what you mean.

Cici is this matted mess of an Old English Sheepdog that delivers a litter of pups less than a week after you bring her home. Ten puppies, to be exact. There are plenty of pictures of Cici, her pups, and you sitting on the front porch of the single-wide trailer home and playing in the snow.

Not that you remember any of it.

But then comes Scrappy. Grandma Audrey breeds and raises and sells Boston terriers. She takes it so seriously she holds a wedding ceremony for her dame and sire. Mitzie wears a tutu, and she clips a bowtie to Buster's collar.

Grandma can't sell Scrappy. He's tiger-striped brindle, not black and white. He's bigger than all his brothers and sisters, too. Too big, according to the breed standard. And he's always fighting, so Grandma names him Scrappy, like Scooby-Doo's nephew.

When you go to live with Grandma, Scrappy sleeps in your bed. While picking strawberries down by the boathouse, Scrappy comes up over the hill when Grandma calls your name. From that, she knows where you are and that you're all right. When he comes flying down the dirt road and up onto the cabin porch and scratches at the screen door enough to tear it open and crawl through to get to her, Grandma knows something is wrong. And she's right. A black bear is chasing you and the buckets of berries you won't put down. She saves the day by clanging some pots and pans together, without ever leaving the porch.

When you sit with the soles of your feet kissing the rippling waves working their way toward shore, waiting for one of the sunfish to bite, a lone wolf walks out of the woods and stands between you and the cabin. Scrappy issues from the ether with hair raised and runs it off. When you start school, he howls the entire first day until you step back onto the stoop. Every day after, he sleeps on the mat in the mudroom waiting for four o'clock. The one time he isn't waiting is the day he dies from a series of violent seizures on the way to the vet's office. You don't get to say goodbye, but you can always run your fingers along the passenger side of the dashboard in Grandpa's Chevy Impala station wagon, where Debbie sat with him on his last car ride when he seized and then came to and then seized again and came to again until he didn't come to anymore. He left bite marks in the pleather and foam of the dashboard, still trying to fight, not wanting to say goodbye until you came home from school.

The class spent the day at the Duluth Depot on a field trip. You come home bursting with excitement about all the things you saw at the museum. But what you don't see makes you forget all the things you did see. Scrappy isn't sitting in the sun next to the mail slot waiting for you. Instead, you see Dad and Grandma standing in the kitchen. The closer you get to them, the more of the family you see waiting.

"Where is Scrappy?" you say.

No one answers.

Dad pulls out the step stool from behind the garbage can and tells you to sit down. It's the same step stool he sat down on when he tried to teach you how to tie your shoe. Dad kept telling you something about a rabbit and a tree and the rabbit going down into the hole and slapping you each time you messed it up because you weren't grasping what he was saying because his hand hung down at his side, hovering right over your head. So he had to keep slapping you off the stool and down onto the floor until you got it right. But you stopped getting up off the floor, and since you couldn't seem to learn something so simple, he bought you a pair of Blue Light Special Velcro shoes instead. A simple enough solution. When you wore them, the other kids teased you and picked on you and pushed you around on the playground. But you got beat up enough at home and weren't having it at school too. Remember the crowd of kids who gathered around? Remember their chant?

Fight

Fight

Who is the nigger?

Who is the white?

Remember coming home and showing Grandma the white slip you got for fighting? While she read it aloud, Dad put his coffee cup down and looked at you, seeing the obvious signs of a struggle, and asked if you won. When you do win a fight, he leaves you alone, goes back to his coffee without laying a hand on you. Like today.

So, once more, sitting on the step stool, you look up at them and ask, "Where is Scrappy?"

Someone says, "He went to sleep," and you glare at Dad with shiny eyes and ask, "Why?" and he says, "It's okay to cry. It's okay."

But it's not okay. When it comes to Dad and anything with four legs and fur, it's not okay.

See, one night, he staggered after Debbie, chasing her from room to room with his leather belt in hand. This belt has dueling rows of steel grommets running the length of the entire thing, end to end, from the fold to the tip. Think seventies biker apparel.

He loves that belt.

He loves how it leaves perfect little rows of welts.

He loves to fold it in half and snap it.

He loves how the sound makes you jump and whimper in anticipation.

He loves to feel the warmth of the leather in his hand once he's done.

It's a point of pride for him to crack it hard enough to make flesh poke through the center of the grommets for a fraction of a second, like Grandma and the wooden spoon with a hole in it.

Debbie darts into the back bedroom and hides beneath Mom and Dad's oak-framed king-sized bed. By her side is her tiny teacup poodle, defending her, baring its teeth, growling, snapping at a hand twice its size lunging at the both of them under the bed.

In the interest of turning minutes into seconds, the dog becomes too brazen and charges too close, and he snatches it up. And with dog in hand, yelping for someone to help, Dad belches out, "Get out from under that bed, little girl."

But Debbie silently protests.

For him, there is no counting to ten, or even three. He doesn't do all that. Instead, he flings the tiny teacup poodle against the far wall of the trailer's back bedroom. It lets out one final yelp while falling to the floor, where the rest of its breath leaves its lungs. Or maybe it yelps while flying through the air, toward the wall. Or maybe it happens so fast that it happens all in the same second, and the sound simply hangs in the air while it's still falling to the floor, like a gunshot that drops a deer instantly.

Either way, he warned her.

She makes sure to stay beneath the bed until his boots leave the room and their clomping stops shaking the single-wide, and all she can hear is his telltale snoring echoing back down the hallway. She doesn't dare reach a hand out from beneath the bed to stroke her dog's fur one last time. She doesn't know what to do. Most children would never think to hide beneath a bed to escape a monster. It's not a typical childhood lesson, but neither is *let sleeping dogs lie.*

There is this other dog, Midget. She's the runt of her litter. Grandma can't get rid of her either, so she has to keep her, too.

One rainy day at the cabin, you want to play with the dogs, so you power slide on the carpet and pet Midget with your face almost touching hers and blurt out something meant to wake her, and it works. She lets out a warning, one you do not heed, which causes her to latch onto your lower lip, which causes you to jump to your feet with her still clamped on.

Your bellowing summons Dad first, followed by Grandma. Before she can intervene, he hurls Midget up against the living room wall like someone is trying to steal second base. She doesn't die, but she hits the wall so hard an eye burst out of her head. The sound she makes can't be unheard. The things Grandma says to Dad while holding Midget in one hand and her eyeball in the other were of the sort that those within earshot let fall on deaf ears.

The next summer, Debbie's cat, Tippy, doesn't come to the cabin. She got old. She stays at Grandma's house instead, and Dad makes sure she has food and water. It's your job to make sure she has a clean shitbox, Dad says. The summer before, you and the rest of the grandkids watched her kill a weasel while you dined on corn dogs and grilled cheese sandwiches, which you called *girl cheese* for far too long, which you eventually refused to eat, once you decided you didn't want a snack meant for girls.

Like Tippy, you didn't go to the cabin that summer either. You'd moved in with Dad a few weeks before, the summer after you finished the sixth grade, right before you began the seventh.

Dad guesses Tippy won't see the end of summer and sends you to find where she's taken to hiding.

She's warming herself beneath the television set. You only see the white of her fur, really, but you tell Dad, "Here she is. She's under here."

He hoists up the TV to see for himself and grunts in affirmation. This TV of Grandma's is one of those big wooden bastards that come up to your belly button and lets go a clunk, clunk, clunk when you change the channels from three to six to eight to ten.

Dad plops the TV back down while you're out in the kitchen, and Tippy lets out an exhausted meow. A day or so later, you ask when you should check on her again, and he explains, "She's dead," without offering anything more on the matter.

That same summer, when the neighborhood sees a spike in skunks and raccoons ravaging trash cans and dumpsters as well as coyotes killing dogs left leashed to back porches, you see Dad come up with a cure. He takes a bottle of aspirin, crushes it up, mixes it into a pound of raw hamburger, and makes a batch of meatballs. But they don't go into the oven. Oh, and he puts a treble hook in the center of each meatball before tossing them here and there along the alleyway. Problem solved. No more dumped over trash cans. No more bloody dog collars left dangling. None of this should surprise you.

When a second cousin can't afford to have the vet dock the tails of a litter of pups, you stand in the driveway with Sam and watch while Dad takes the box of them to the woods and does it himself. He uses a pistol to take off the tails. He tells the two of you the bullets sever and cauterize the wound all at once.

He even brings along a tub of Vaseline for show.

Little details like that make a lie seem more plausible. But the truth of it is the cousin couldn't get rid of the pups or afford to feed all of them, and they were too smart to wander into the pigpen the way the last litter of kittens did. Dogs aren't always so bright. Remember Porky, the Cocker Spaniel Dad took in from your cousin, Denise, after she found out her new landlord didn't allow dogs? Porky got into an ice cream bucket full of used antifreeze Dad kept under the kitchen sink.

"Dogs love it. It smells sweet to them."

Dad volunteers that last little bit of information to Grandma and whoever cares to listen before returning to his cup of coffee, while everyone else in the room looks at each other, wondering *who the hell keeps a bucket of used antifreeze under their kitchen sink?* It's a safe bet he did the math and figured a jug of antifreeze is a lot cheaper than a bag of dog food. Even the bright yellow bag that says DOG FOOD in big black letters. He's like a five-year-old who can't quite grasp how outlandish the tales he tells sound. It doesn't take long for you to notice how almost every time he opens his mouth, Grandma takes a drag off her cigarette and stares the way a defeated mother does while sitting behind her son on an episode of Court TV.

There's another time, a time before you got cable, a time when the phone is still tethered to the wall, a time long after Mom and Dad divorced, a time long after Debbie moved out on her own. There's no one else there that day, a day that worms its way into your memories for two reasons. Both disturb you in their own special way. First, it's the day Dad lets you, his son—a tender thirteen years of age—watch *The Rocky Horror Picture Show* while you sit in your respective recliners eating microwaved Banquet chicken and instant mashed potatoes and whole-kernel canned corn from faux wooden TV trays.

The two of you hear a sound come from the kitchen, one that doesn't raise a question as to what is happening, one that causes Dad to shove his TV tray to the side, accompanied by a melodramatic "Goddamn it!"

Dad hates Slater, your Japanese Bobtail cat, who gets his name from you watching *Pump up the Volume* and *Gleaming the Cube* and *Heathers* too many times. Slater doesn't make much of a dent in the breaded chicken breast he's helped himself to atop the kitchen table, but the whole box is covered in his hair, so Dad bashes his head against the tabletop, cursing him in cadence with each successive smack until he goes limp in Dad's hands and lets go a low, haunting yowl.

Dad's back fills the entire doorway, and you stand behind him with fists clenched until he stomps up the stairs and tosses Slater into the cage, where he lands in the litter box.

You're still standing there, fixated on the baseball bat balanced against the wall between the refrigerator and the back door, when he comes down the stairs and tells you not to let Slater out of his cage for a week. "Maybe then he'll learn some table manners," he says, and pushes play on the remote and stuffs his face with what's left on his plate.

Sometime during the night, Slater's tongue slides out of his mouth and turns white. He feels cold to the touch. Stiff too. When you tell Dad how you found him, you watch him throw what was once your cat into a plastic bag, which he tells you to toss into the dumpster out back of the building on the way to school.

That would have been the fall of 1990, the year the Jim Belushi movie *K-9* came out on VHS. That year, Dad became obsessed with the idea of owning a German Shepherd, and as luck would have it, one of his drinking buddies, Bob-the-Dog-Catcher, says he has one locked up down at the pound. A runner. A repeat customer. He can have it.

The next day, the two of you climb into Dad's two-tone, brown and beige, four-door Reliant and head down to the pound to pick him up. On the way, Dad's voice booms between songs, saying he has the perfect name for him: Jerry Lee. Of course you knew that, you saw it coming, you mouthed it when he said it. What else would he call a German Shepherd after wearing out two different copies of that damn movie?

Rin Tin Tin doesn't have quite the same ring to Dad as it once did.

Bob-the-Dog-Catcher hands you a leash and collar from a box filled with leashes and collars that once belonged to dogs he never found homes for and put to sleep.

"The dog's in the back," he says. "Death row," he mumbles to your father before they go back to bullshitting.

You walk by little scraggly, yappy things, a couple of lab mixes, a few different dogs obviously crossed with huskies and malamutes or whatever those sled dogs are, something that looks like the Hound of the Baskervilles, but no German Shepherds. Then you head toward the cages at the opposite end of the building, where the lights are off.

He's not a German Shepherd. He's not brown with a black mask and saddle. He doesn't have the sloped back and those hindquarters that always look like they are crouched, ready to pounce, like you see on all the cop shows. He's a blonde Brutus. His back comes up to your hip, and when he lifts his head, he can stare you right in the face.

"He's a—fucking—wolf," you tell Dad and Bob-the-Dog-Catcher, whispering when you say "fucking," not wanting to get hit, but wanting them to take you seriously.

"Nah, he's a gold color," Bob-the-Dog-Catcher says. "Don't know what all he is. He's Shepherd, though. Go see, Dick. Take him for a walk, David."

"Walk?" you say. "Like, open the cage?"

Dad doesn't walk him any farther than the back door of the car. Maybe it's because the dog pound sits across the street from the shit plant, or it could have to do with his mind being made up sight unseen. Jerry Lee takes a dump in the side yard as soon as he jumps out of the back seat of the sedan. Dad tells you to pick it up and takes Jerry Lee inside to show him the house.

The spade shovel isn't big enough to do the job, so you take two trips across the street into the woods of the abandoned block and fling the shit into the overgrown brush.

Meanwhile, Jerry Lee makes your home his home. He climbs into your recliner. It's too small for him, so he spends the next hour sniffing every inch of the downstairs: the bags of trash, the pile of laundry yet to make it into the washing machine, the two recliners, Dad's boots, the black shiny sheen on the kitchen carpet leading from the back door to the sink before it forms a Y and heads past the stove and into the next room, giving way to the brown, beige, and gold shag on the living room floor and walls. He smells the things that shouldn't have a smell but do because they still smell of Slater.

It takes some time for him to stumble onto the spiraled steps that lead to the second floor, where he finds the two bedrooms and the bathroom. He laps a drink or two out of the calcified toilet bowl before making it from Dad's room to the spare bedroom. You can hear all this, along with his nails clinking on the concrete through the register. He seems at home until the two of you hear a heaving of metal and the sound of something falling apart. The sound makes you look out the window, thinking he made it out onto the overhang.

His being a runner makes you a runner, too. You rush up the steps faster than you should. The vinyl treads are slick, moist, damp from the humidity that never escapes the house, and you should know this. For your forgetfulness, you nearly faceplant on the steps.

Jerry Lee lies in the center of the camping cot you use for a bed, making it sag, almost touching the floor. A few springs are missing, shot across the spare bedroom, lost in the piles of things Dad doesn't want to look at or throw away. From the top of the stairs, some of the metal straps look bent, useless—even if you can manage to find the springs— so you holler out for Dad and wait for him to climb the stairs. When he sees what you see, he says, "Well, shit, guess we'll have to find a bed now," and he finds a monstrosity of a brass bed someone spray-painted a dark chocolate-looking shade of brown.

Time and time again, you wake, folded in two, with Jerry Lee standing with his four paws teetering on your stomach the way a circus elephant balances atop a ball for all the ladies and gentlemen, boys and girls, children of all ages. Jerry Lee stares into your eyes and waits to hear Dad bellow out, "Take him outside!" losing all semblance of calm once he hears "outside" travel up through the register.

It doesn't take much imagination to realize Dad sends Jerry Lee upstairs and waits to hear you groan so he doesn't have to get up from his recliner or leave his cup of coffee, or whatever he's using to lubricate himself. You slip on some shoes and try to make it to the bathroom, but when a dog that outweighs you shepherds you down the stairs, the two of you take your morning piss on the same tree.

You can't keep up when the morning walk turns into the morning run. Sometimes the leash rips right out of your hand, which gives you an idea: skeetching.

Skeetching is when a skateboarder trails behind a car, clutching onto the bumper. The only difference is that you'll be holding onto Jerry Lee's leash, sailing down the fresh blacktop the county used to pave Idaho Street. There's not much of a straightaway until you get alongside the woods that serve as a buffer for the abandoned steel mill turned abandoned coke plant. It's mostly a curved road circumnavigating Morgan Park, which has a horseshoe shape to it, with a river wrapping around the town the way the Mississippi does with the crescent-shaped city of New Orleans.

Idaho can be a busy street. But if you look up the top speeds of a timber wolf and a German Shepherd, you'll see there's no reason for anyone to bitch when the two of you are barreling down the middle of the street at close to forty miles an hour, when it is posted for thirty.

You take Jerry Lee out the back door and grab your skateboard, along with the ten to twelve feet of leftover rope from when Dad cut a new anchor line. Then it's a straight shot toward the bridge, past the Lutheran home for bad kids, where you wait for a lull in traffic. Once the city bus passes, you look toward the bridge, crouching a little to see all the way to the highway. It's clear, so you slide the tail of the skateboard off the curb and push the nose to the left and right until it gets rolling pretty good and Jerry Lee trots alongside. You shove the nose left and right and get going even faster, a cue he takes to mean you want him to take the slack out of the rope and run. The board begins to wobble once he gets up to speed, the kind of wobbling which happens right before a skater eats shit. But you get low on the board, and everything balances out.

The two of you make it to Ninety-Second Street, the other side of the abandoned block that separates your block from the Lutheran home for bad kids. By then, Jerry Lee is in a full sprint and the skateboard wheels are howling. Then you come up to Ninety-First Street, your street, and look left for Dad or Dad's car, so it's a safe bet he hasn't budged from his recliner. When you look back to see where you and Jerry Lee are headed, you know the straightaway is less than a block away, so you get a little lower and lean forward a little. That's right about the time a rabbit comes hightailing it out of the alleyway, across Idaho, and into the woods that serve as a buffer for the abandoned steel mill turned abandoned coke plant.

Jerry Lee follows and sends the skateboard off into the grass while you skid along the fresh blacktop. It's where you got the matching oval-shaped scars on your left knee and elbow, neither of which ever go away.

Luckily, Jerry Lee is just enough German Shepherd to get stuck in the thicket of briars and broken branches and dead saplings that got choked out by the bigger birch trees and poplars. So you find him searching spastically for a way deeper in—once you peel your bloodied self off Idaho, that is.

Your jeans are ripped, but not in the post–hair band eighties, pre-grunge band nineties kind of way. The blood comes out of the shirt, but the thorns and thistles you weave through to get to Jerry Lee turn your shirt into something Dad uses when he needs to check the oil in his car.

You tell Dad, "Jerry Lee saw a rabbit," without mentioning the skateboard, and Dad laughs and tells you where the hydrogen peroxide is.

Walking Jerry Lee doesn't always involve a wardrobe change. He's a great wingman. Neighborhood girls come outside to pet him. Sometimes this turns a walk around the block into an hour-long affair. At night, you don't even have to watch where you're going; people just get out of your way. And when Dad doesn't come home, Jerry Lee lies at the foot of the bed, staring at the bedroom doorway while you sleep. It's easy enough to picture Jerry Lee doing the same thing after the school nurse sends you home, right before Christmas break, with pneumonia.

Dad won't pick you up since it's only a two-block walk, so when you make it through the door, he points to a pint glass sitting on the TV tray and says, "Drink that, then go to bed. Don't get me sick," without ever taking his eyes off the screen.

When you wake up and stumble back down the stairs, there's a plastic bag sitting in the empty recliner, tied in an impossible knot. You pick it up and take a seat, and before you can ask, Dad says, "Merry Christmas," which makes you squint at the calendar tacked to the closet door on the other side of the living room.

Your eyes are still fuzzy, your head is pounding, but you no longer have flu-like symptoms. "What'd you give me?" you say, closing your eyes against the blinding light of the table lamp.

"Open it and find out."

"No. To drink."

"Oh. Wild Turkey," he says. "Same thing we put in your baby bottle when you were teething."

You tear the bag open to find a pair of shoes tied to one another with the laces knotted, no box. Displays sold as Blue Light Specials, in other words. A pair of knockoff British Knights.

"For track, in the spring," Dad says.

You run the hundred-meter hurdles, the high jump, and the long jump. The long jump is your bread and butter. You manage to jump sixteen feet and eight inches one day during practice and run home to tell Dad what the coach told you, that it's a record for junior high boys in this region. Dad says, "What's the high school record? Tell me when you beat that. Now, sprint to the fridge and grab me a beer." He laughs until you hand him his beer, but you stop going to track practice.

Instead, you pick away, trying to make your way through guitar tablatures you've pulled out of the dumpster at the gas station until you break a string, and then Dad won't buy you more because "You'll just break them again." Instead, you shovel two hundred dollars' worth of snow and buy your own guitar.

The next spring, Jerry Lee isn't standing in the kitchen, waiting to see who is messing with the lock when you come home from practice. He's not in the living room either, lying between the recliners like he sometimes does when he's home alone. He's not plopped down on your bed. He's lying on the bedroom floor gnawing on a baseball like it's the leg of a felled deer and he wants the marrow. He has the Kirby Puckett pop fly ball you caught during the 1987 season playoffs. The ball fell from your hand and got scooped up by a grown man from the next section over. You stood there, staring at the man while he went back to his seat. Then someone yelled, "Give it to the kid," and, after two or three iterations, it turned into the whole section chanting, "Give it to the kid," until he did give it to the kid.

Jerry Lee ripped the stitching and peeled the leather off the baseball. You don't yell, "No!" or "Stop!"—you fall on top of him, punch him, try to pry it from his jaws, trying to get him to give it to the kid. But nothing will get him to give up the ball. You keep wailing on him until he yelps and whimpers. The ball is ruined, but you keep wailing away until you feel yourself float up into the air. You make sure to kick him in the head before you float too far away. Even if it's only a tap with the toe of your shoes.

The air grows stagnant when you float up toward the ceiling. The air is heavy with the smell of sweat and stale beer and baby powder and Brylcreem: Dad.

He's bear-hugging you, pinning your arms to your sides, squeezing the air from your chest. He pulls you out of the spare bedroom and wrestles you down the stairs to the kitchen. But he never hits you. He plops you down in the chair and says, "You can't—" trying to catch a breath, pointing upstairs to where Jerry Lee is, "You can't do that."

He gets no response from you, but keeps on talking.

"Jesus Christ, you can't do that. Don't make me a complete failure," he huffs, still trying to catch his breath. With wet eyes stinging from his sweat dripping from his brow, he says, "At least let me be an example of what not to be."

Jerry Lee is just enough German Shepherd to become affected by hip dysplasia, causing crippling lameness and painful arthritis. By the next spring, he's not a runner anymore. You are. You try out for track again and fall in with the long-distance runners. At five foot nine, your stride is longer than most other boys in junior high.

On the second or third day of track practice, the pack of long-distance runners is sent out to run a mile-long loop around the school. From Eighty-Eighth Street, the group heads toward the abandoned steel mill turned abandoned coke plant. Then they turn right to where Eighty-Eighth turns into Idaho Street. On Idaho Street, everyone takes turns leading the pack, leapfrogging the whole way, switching each time they pass an intersection: Eighty-Ninth Street, Ninetieth Street, and again on Ninety-First Street, where you see Bob-the-Dog-Catcher's Animal Control truck parked in front of the house.

You slow the pace, slide to the back of the pack and watch Bob-the-Dog-Catcher and Dad come out the front door carrying Jerry Lee toward the back of the Animal Control truck. Right then, the pack slips behind the trees and overgrowth of the abandoned block separating Ninety-First Street from the Lutheran home for bad kids. Right then is when you lose your wind, get a cramp in your calf, get a stitch in your side, wave the team on when they look back, tell them you need to walk the rest of the way.

Jerry Lee's leash and collar are going back into the box of leashes and collars that once belonged to dogs Bob-the-Dog-Catcher never found homes for and put to sleep.

Dad didn't want you to see Jerry Lee leave like that. He didn't want you to be home when it happened. He doesn't want to be home when you come home and there is no more Jerry Lee. He doesn't know how to be that kind of dad. He's only good at fathering children.

That much he knows.

FISHING IN THE DARK

DJ Jazzy Jeff & the Fresh Prince thwump out of Glen's boombox speakers. The two of you stomp your feet along with the bass, sending ripples across the otherwise calm lake.

It's one of those especially hot days when Grandma wears her one-piece swimsuit, the brown and beige one with leaves and flowers on it, the one that looks a lot like the couch cushions. All the adults sit in the shade of the cabin's screened-in porch, sweltering, cooling themselves with Grasshoppers: a concoction made from crème de menthe, crème de cacao, and Schwan's French vanilla ice cream.

The two of you are twelve and nine—too old for bobber fishing—so you cast and rap along with the cassette about how parents just don't understand and reel lures in faster than any fish could swim. But being out in the boat on the lake is the summertime neutral zone—kind of like how the couch and coffee table were safe while the carpet was lava, back when Grandma went to ceramics on Wednesday nights and Grandpa let you be a kid for once.

After changing lures out three different times, you conclude it's the boombox, on the bottom of the boat, scaring the fish away. Neither of you wants to head back to the cabin. Instead, the two of you want to see who can cast the farthest.

Of course, there's some cheating, but it's not really cheating when there aren't any rules, so you swap out the Hula Popper for a Dardevle spoon meant for muskies, which is damn near too heavy for the five-pound test line, considering your knotting talents. You can't really call it winning either, considering you lose your grip and get to watch the rod and reel sail through the air and plunge down into the lake.

The bay echoes your "Fuck—" back to you. Glen adds a chuckle to his. You do not. His laugh is a nervous one, knowing full well the ass beating coming your way once you make shore.

You contemplate rowing over to the nearest dock, dropping off Glen, living out your days in the boat. At least until the lake freezes. Then they can walk out and get you. So that won't work. You lost Dad's fishing rod in the lake. *Minnesota* means cloudy water, after all.

Lost it is.

Glen agreed to tell his uncle about the rod and reel, but the tradeoff is you'll have to row the boat all the way back to the cabin—which you do, staring at Dad's Evinrude motor the whole time, cursing the building blisters. Glen gets out of the boat, says a silent prayer for you, heads up to the cabin to deliver the news. You sit there and never once loosen your grip on the oars. You sit, twisting your wrists, readying yourself, waiting for someone to summon you up to the screened-in front porch of the cabin.

Dad doesn't say much when Glen tells him what you did. Rather than exploding, he takes down the beer he's nursing and fishes his tackle box and a spare rod and reel out of Grandma's boathouse on the way down to the water. You feel him lift the bow off the sand and shove the boat out with a flick of the wrist. He hurdles over you on his way to the back of the boat to claim his seat next to the motor. He doesn't have any desire to discuss your fuckup with you, so he sits and glares out of the corner of his eye.

Rowing the boat back to where you'd lost the rod and reel is easy enough. The spot was directly between the two docks on the other side of the big weed bed.

Dad laughs and tells Glen the music, and you banging your feet on the bottom of the boat, scared all the fish to the other side of the lake. Lunkerville. He'll be going over there as soon as he gets his rod and reel back. "Whole lake could hear you dingbats," he says to Glen and pulls a deep-running lure from the bottom of his tackle box, snapping it onto his leader.

The treble hook dangling from his lure looks big enough to work as an anchor.

Dad casts his line way out and sets the reel with a whir, thwump, click, and goes back to glaring at you, still saying nothing. There's nothing to say. He has no time for you. He's merely waiting for the lure to sink down to the bottom, waiting for it to sink into your thick skull what'll happen to you once you're back on shore.

Though there's no question in your mind what'll happen.

When he figures out his lure is laying down in the sand and silt and loon shit, he reels his line back in real slow-like and shakes his head from side to side just as slowly, like he's contemplating whether to give you the belt or let Grandma grab the flyswatter. Either way, the rest of the day will be spent with blistered butt cheeks in the bottom of the bunk bed.

Your only escape will come when you get brave enough to ask to go to the outhouse. Dinner, too. But you'll have to listen to them, dishing out ice cream and popping popcorn. You won't be able to turn on the light to read or color, so you'll have to use the sliver of light coming under the door to make sure you stay between the lines once the sun sets. God help you if Grandma finds another page where you've gone outside the lines, wasted her money.

Dad's line snags, and the tip of his pole dips down toward the water, making the air in your lungs go icy. The longer it takes to get his rod and reel back from the bottom of the lake, the more pissed he'll get, and the worse the beating will be. Call it causality. If he snaps the line and loses another leader and lure, you'll get it even worse than what's already coming.

But he doesn't bother trying to free his lure from the snag by letting out his line or lifting his rod up in the air, slow and steady, like how he taught you. Instead, he keeps reeling back in—slower now. His rod tip bends lower and lower with each turn of the reel. When it touches the water, he lifts the spare rod over his head, and his rod comes up with it—caked in mud and loon shit and weeds, but the line and lure and reel are all still there.

One single, solitary cast, and he brought it up from the bottom of the lake. Dad doesn't look the least bit surprised. Glen's face is frozen in a look of *Holy Shit, Uncle Dickie.* Your face is frozen too. How the hell are you supposed to react to something like that? You don't. You sit while Dad undoes his lure from his leader, puts it back into his tackle box, and wait to get cuffed upside the head hard enough to dive into the water.

Glen sings Dad's praises the whole time you row the boat back to shore. You don't open your mouth. You're wondering if you'll be able to slip into the bedroom and stuff a coloring book into the back of your pants to soften the blow. But he's probably too sober to fall for that.

Glen hops out of the boat and pulls the bow onto shore again, and waits, says nothing, stands statue. He knows his Uncle Dickie is perturbed and knows not to provoke him. Glen doesn't want to get in the way if Dad decides to beat your ass right there on the shore. Nor does he dare leave until he's told, but he's got one foot pointed in the direction of the cabin—he's ready to run when the moment comes.

When you stand up with the rod and reel, Dad barks out, "David!" from the back of the boat. You almost wet yourself. When you turn to face him, he hands you a handful of bobbers. For you, it's two handfuls. Some fall to the bottom of the boat, but you don't have time to pick them up before he tells Glen to push the boat out and get in.

They leave you there on the beach and go to the other side of the lake, Lunkerville. Grandma calls you inside for lunch. Grandpa makes like he's handing you a cup of water in one of those bright blue aluminum Bascal tumblers, but he's decided you need a Grasshopper too.

NICE BIKE

Every so often, Grandpa Bub picks you up from school. You get to sit in the front and see where you're going, which is nice. But it's not as memorable as the other stuff.

First, like when you walk through the front door of the house, he says, "What did you learn in school today?"—but in the car alone with Grandpa, it's not punctuated by Grandma Audrey's trilled, "Get your ass in the kitchen and do your schoolwork."

Instead, he listens while you ramble on about your lessons.

Second, he'll yell things out the car window, like, "Little girl, your bike is broken!" and wait for her to hop off the bicycle and give it a once-over before he continues, telling her, "Your *back* wheel is going *forward*." He'll put on his hazards and wait until his logic works its way into her ear and out the other. When her face lets him know she's convinced something is wrong, something she can't fix, he recommends she push her bike home and tell her dad he needs to fix it before she gets hurt. Then he puts it back into drive and does that yuck-yuck-yuck laugh of his and says, "Oh, what a schmuck."

He calls everyone a schmuck.

The dictionary defines schmuck as an annoying person. The Yiddish dictionary says it's another word for the penis. But a Jewish friend tells you it's the word for the leftover skin that's tossed away after a circumcision.

You don't ever take your bike to school; it's only a three-block walk. The first bike you can recall is painted red, white, and blue, with shooting stars running along the frame, like something Evel Knievel would ride as a child. The tires are made of solid rubber. It's impossible for you to pop a tire. It's impossible to pop a wheelie, too. The bike is so heavy you can't get it up off the ground no matter how hard you yank up on the handlebars. And those solid rubber tires aren't made of soft rubber, either. They're so hard you can feel every pebble you roll over, every crack in the sidewalk, every bit of gravel in the concrete.

The vibrations rattle your bones and blur your vision. Because of this, you wobble so bad it looks like you can't figure out how to handle a two-wheeler until you figure out to ride through everyone's front lawns, which pisses off some otherwise friendly neighbors.

The bike after that kind of shows up one day. It's built by Glen. He has dozens of different bikes piled up alongside Aunt Bobbie's garage. The cops come and look over the collection every so often, trying to find a bike someone reported missing. But he never stole one. There's no stars or stickers on the bike he gives you. It's painted a matte blue primer color. It's blue, so it must be a boy's bike—never mind the tassels hanging down from the ape-hanger handlebars, or the white vinyl banana seat with daisies on it, held high into the air with the sissy bar. The tassels come off with one merciless tug, and if your butt stays planted on the seat, no one will see the flowers. The ape-hangers would be cool if it was 1975 or so, but it's 1985 or so, so you pretend you're a biker riding around on a chopper and no one really says anything. Though, it is kind of hard to pull off that biker thing while wearing a pair of basketball shorts along with an *I Celebrated My Birthday at Chuck E. Cheese's* T-shirt that Grandma got for you at Goodwill. Those shorts, especially, were a bad idea. They are way too slippery to wear when riding on a vinyl seat.

Remember the massive tree sitting in the center of the block. The roots run under the sidewalk, making a killer jump. One day, the wind is blowing just right at your back, you get going super fast, and launch right into the air, and slide right off the back of the banana seat and bounce onto the back tire.

That's when you realize your back wheel is going forward, too, and your tighty-whities aren't quite tight enough to stop your ball sack from getting dragged by the back tire into the frame.

No one notices you, or if they do, they don't come to check on you. No one asks if you're okay. If they saw what happened, they know you're not. If anyone heard what happened, they would have heard a sound that made birds take flight. Alone, you lie on someone's front lawn with a little vomit on your lips and tears in your eyes, along with some presumable snot dripping from your nose. From there, you listen to the wind in the trees, smell the pine needles on the ground beneath you, along with the fresh-cut grass, try to process how the hell it even happened, wonder whether you're a girl now.

The bike after that comes from Mom, once she gets brave enough to come around on the regular. It's a bright red Huffy racing bike with hand brakes and foot pegs on the front forks. A pad Velcroes onto the frame to soften the blow if you fall when doing an endo. There's another on the handlebars to save your teeth from shattering. But, really, it's more of a cushion for your friend's butt cheeks when they're balancing on the handlebars. The tires are made of white rubber. Nobody else in the neighborhood has white tires. The only other place anyone has ever seen those is on the TV, but it doesn't have the mag wheels like the BMX racers do. Instead, it has these white plastic aero discs covering the spokes.

You can see it from a mile away in the summer sun.

No one ever thought to buy a chain and padlock. You'd pedal around the neighborhood and see bikes in a pile in someone's front yard. No one knew anyone's phone number, but everyone knew which bike belonged to what kid. So, when someone says someone else has your bike, you break into a full sprint toward his house, and when he sees you walk into his yard, he comes flying outside to meet you. And you freeze.

He's a head taller than you. He's been held back. This isn't the first time he's taken something of yours, so you back off his lawn and head home.

Grandpa Bub asks, "Where'd you leave your bike?"

"Someone took it," you tell him.

"Who?" he says, his words accompanied by a jingling of car keys. He calls out to Grandma, "Auddie, I'm going out."

From behind the steering wheel, he asks again where your bike is, and you answer: "Dan took it."

"Where's Dan live?" he asks and puts the car into drive.

"Up above Eighth."

Up above Eighth, you point to Dan's avenue and tell Grandpa it's the last house, but he can see the bike as soon as he turns the corner, and he guns it up the hill to the dead end and says, "Go get your bike."

You slink out of the passenger seat and close the door as quietly as possible, but Grandpa's brakes squeal when the car comes to a stop, so Dan's already watching from the front window. By the time you grab hold of your bike, he yanks it out of your hands and sneers at you.

Then his eyes widen in a way you've never seen before.

You're surrounded in shadow—as if a giant cloud moved overhead—and you concede the bike isn't yours anymore.

Grandpa Bub is a six-foot-six Swede who has worked with steel since the time he came home from WWII, so what he does next is like watching an elderly Larry Bird swat a basketball out of someone's hands—if those hands were Dan's shoulders.

You come up to about the elbow on Grandpa, which makes it easy for him to reach right over the top of your head and slap Dan with an open palm. Dan's basketball of a head looks like it loses some air when it meets the soft dirt of his front yard. You wonder which hurt worse: the slap itself or kissing the turf. Grandpa Bub's hands are so leathery from working at the tool factory for forty-plus years, he can cup his hands together and play "Amazing Grace" with the escaping air. It's a safe bet his hand didn't tingle the slightest bit.

You don't remember Grandpa putting the bike into the back of the station wagon. There's only an embedded image of the giant gap between Dan's two front teeth, along with his swollen lips and his greasy, stringy hair, as he looks up at you from the dirt. And you know you don't have to be afraid of him again.

KINDERGARTEN

KIDS WITH LATE FALL BIRTHDAYS sometimes wait another year to start school, but they let you in—despite the class being full. It's a safe bet they get a sense of how burned out Grandma Audrey is. She's taken to grounding you for almost any reason as soon as her patience runs out. Most mornings, that's right after her coffee cup goes dry. She takes her coffee black, no cream, no sugar, but she likes light roast, so you can never tell when she makes the switch over to brandy. The color is identical, and her slurring sounds a lot like when her false teeth slide out of her head after she warms her cup in the microwave a tad too long.

The principal lives across the street, giving her a front-row seat to the morning routine. In the summer, you wake, eat a bowl of cereal, after which Grandma sends you outside, latching the door behind you. Later, she'll scream your name to let you know there's lunch on the front stoop. If you don't get there before the squirrels or whatever stray might be running around the neighborhood that day, then it's just too damn bad, huh?

Unless it's raining, really raining, the only way to go inside is if you need to poop. There is a storm drain between Grandma's and the neighbor's house for number one.

When it does really rain, the day consists of cornflakes, *$25,000 Pyramid, Family Feud, Hollywood Squares, The Price Is Right,* then soaps: *The Young and the Restless, The Bold and the Beautiful, Guiding Light, As the World Turns,* and *General Hospital.*

That's if you keep quiet.

Otherwise, she'll send you upstairs to your bedroom, and if you get too loud up there, you'll get to clean the basement. The basement is unfinished, meaning its walls are damp from the time when the snow melts until it falls again. When the toilet flushes, the water rushes through the manhole before heading to the city sewer. It's covered, but it's not exactly airtight, so there's a smell.

The basement houses a washer, dryer, freezer, and the fruit room. The fruit room is where Grandma keeps all her canned goods and jars of tomatoes and jellies in case the Commies come. The basement freezer houses all the Schwan's ice cream delights you're denied, along with the corn dogs and taco burgers and fish fillets Grandma makes when she doesn't feel like cooking from scratch.

The basement is also where the dogs crap all winter long because Grandma refuses to send them outside into the drifting snow. Instead, she sends you downstairs with an ice chipper to scrape the petrified crap off the floor. Someone laid tiles on the floor down there, most of which are cracked and broken by the time the chore is passed to you, so right when you get the ice chipper sliding along the floor, peeling up a nice long curl of concrete dust and dog crap and whatever comes in when the city sewer backs up into the basement, the ice chipper rams against the edge of a broken piece of tile and the handle punches you in the gut, sending slivers into the palms of your hands and you to the floor. You break your fall by putting both hands out in front of you, and your bloodied hands become slathered with damp dog shit and little granules of concrete and whatever comes in when the city sewer lines back up into the basement.

Dizzied from the fall, you stand and crack your head on a low-hanging asbestos-wrapped pipe. This sends a cloud of dust into the air, making you sneeze and cough. You can't stop sneezing, so you blow your nose on your shirt, and Grandma stomps her feet on the dining room floor, hollers about how you sound like a goddamned bull moose, prompting you to tiptoe over to the washtub and rinse your hands off with the scalding hot water which comes from the water heater a few feet away before you head over to the other side of the basement, where you help yourself to some of Schwan's deliciousness.

But if it is summer, and it is really raining, and the city sewer lines back up into the basement, and there's too much noise coming from upstairs, then Grandma gets it in her head you might need to clean your room instead of playing.

This is bad news.

Bad, bad news.

You're to play with one toy at a time. One crayon at a time. There's no taking another out of the box until you've put the one you're using away. The only exceptions are action figures and Lincoln Logs. This makes drag racing the Matchbox cars impossible, which is why you never venture out of the bedroom while playing with them. If you can help it. But if she comes into the bedroom, you're fucked.

And you are fucked.

Two lengths of Matchbox track are clamped onto the nightstand and loop-de-loop toward the foot of the bed before the jump sends cars through the air, over the Incredible Hulk and a succession of monster trucks, landing in the closet where they slide off into the darkness.

Coloring books and crayons are splayed across the floor. GI Joes lie where they fell during their short but honorable fight against the Rebel Alliance. Spider-Man is stalled midway through his ascent to the top bunk, when his batteries drained and died.

When the door swivels open, Grandma Audrey lets go a blood-curdling scream. But blood-curdling doesn't quite capture it. And blood doesn't curdle unless there's an elaborate and lengthy cooking process. Blood caramelizes much easier. Her voice sounds the way a blender does when it's been turned on at too high of a setting and you've forgotten the lid—or maybe you're frozen from fear and can't quite hear, or she's so pissed she can't talk. Luckily, you get your wits about you in time for her to clear the froth from her throat and bark out, "I said clean up your goddamn room!" But you don't move fast enough   even though you're snatching up the crayons so quickly you're snapping and cracking them.

Grandma grabs a handful of hair and lifts you to your knees and looks you in the eyes and says something to you, but her lips are clamped around the filter of a cigarette so tight you can't understand her, so you give her a stupid look and she slams you back to the floor, making you drop the crumbled Crayolas. She mutters, "Pick it up," and you do, and she lifts you again like some sort of yo-yo.

But she's not done.

She doesn't trust you to finish cleaning up on your own. She marches you over to the toy box so fast you can't keep your feet under you. She shakes you and shakes you and shakes you until you figure out to drop it into the toy box. She does this until all the toys are picked up, along with a clump of dog crap you didn't see until she points it out in the back corner of the closet and is convinced it's some Lincoln Logs you were too lazy to put away.

But there is one sunny summer day when it isn't raining, and you do make it to the porch in time to grab lunch before the squirrels or someone's stray dog gets there. Through the screen door, Grandma notices your black hair is becoming bleached by the summer sun, meaning the strawberry-blond hair you got as a birthday gift from your Mick mom is showing through. That just won't do.

Grandma comes back outside, wielding a pair of clippers she got from who-knows-where. She doesn't even let you finish the sandwich, and wasting food is not something she lets slide. She will tell Debbie how there are starving children in Africa without fail when she slows down at the dinner table.

Grandma makes you take a seat on the top step, and she shaves it all off. But Grandpa Bub has had these clippers put away since before they were married, since before she first made him go to Cliff's Barber Shop, since before he began to comb it all to the back and have her cut it with a pair of old kitchen scissors she keeps in the junk drawer.

Regardless of how the clippers are rusted and dulled with age, you have to sit there while she runs the blade through your hair so fast you think she's trying to get it done before the commercial break ends. It sounds the same as when Grandpa runs the lawnmower over the gravel driveway at the cabin. You duck the same too, except it's not because you're afraid of a flying rock, but because some of the hair is coming out by the root.

When she's done, your scalp is bloodied, and you watch the afternoon breeze blow clumps of hair out into the yard and down the street. You see those who've watched this from their front porches and living room windows turn to go back inside or close their curtains.

Your friends are called inside too.

SPLIT CLASS

THE KID NEXT DOOR IS the only one who comes to your birthday party in the first grade. He doesn't get a choice. His mom cuts your hair for free, and Grandma Audrey watches him free of charge in exchange. His mom's hair salon is busiest on Saturday mornings—the day of the party—so he is the one guest who isn't a blood relative.

Every classmate gets an invitation, though, like on Saint Valentine's Day.

It's not only Grandma who the neighborhood kids are afraid of now. Both classes, the first and the second grade, are afraid. But it's a split class. The class being split doesn't mean some are afraid and some aren't, or some are more afraid than others. A split class means the school is so crowded first- and second-graders share a room and a teacher.

It's impossible to keep you segregated, so she combines classes for everything, even quiet time, which is like nap time, but all she does is turn out the lights, and you put your head on the desk for a while. That's when it's the teacher's turn to stare out the window and do nothing—all to the musical stylings of one kid who plays the piano for thirty minutes. "Chariots of Fire" over and again, if memory serves.

All this makes the first grade great, but the second grade redundant. Still, there are times when the teacher needs to separate you: usually when a bored mind cannot be properly busied, so you go out into the hallway until she can decide what she should do with the two of you.

You sit across the hall by the boots and backpacks and snowmobile suits of the kindergarten class, while this other unnamed character sits beneath the construction paper mural made by the whole split class. The mural is a giant purple octopus with a different student's name written inside each of the suction cups glued along the length of the tentacles.

Thanks to thirty-some seven-year-old abstractionists, it looks more like Cthulhu leering down at passersby.

Splayed out all across the granite floor between the two of you are colored pencils, crayons, markers, manila paper, and scissors. Somehow, the conversation turns to mothers. He says, "The octopus is your mom," like he knows you don't know who she is or where she is, or how she could be anybody, even an octopus. Or Cthulhu.

He won't shut up about it, so you throw markers at him, and miss him for the most part. He still won't shut up, so then come the colored pencils. They bounce off the wall behind him or fall short.

The teacher says not to say *shut up*, but *be quiet* doesn't cut it when you really do mean *shut up*, and he still won't zip his lips, so the scissors go next. Then he really won't shut up. He screams *my arm my arm my arm* mixed with *ow ow ow*. Or is it *my mom my mom my mom?* Now he wants his mom and you think *shit shit shit*. Why is it always three? *Yeah yeah yeah*, beginning, middle, and end. But there is no end to his crying, and you know this won't end well because he's being a big baby about the scissors sticking out of his bicep, so you run to his side and do everything to shush him, but he won't stop his bellyaching.

The teacher can't hear his cries courtesy of the concrete walls and her hammering on the upright piano in the back of the classroom, accompanied by the screeching of the songs the class will sing at the Christmas pageant. But you're still fucked.

Ed-the-janitor runs down the hall and sees you standing over some crying kid who is bleeding all over with a pair of scissors sticking out of his arm, so, naturally, you get knocked out of the way and on your ass.

Ed-the-janitor has a flat top haircut—like you do—but his is a salt-and-pepper color. His eyes hide behind the yellow lens of his prescription shooting glasses, so you can't see what color they are—not that pissed off is some sort of eye color. He pounds on Mrs. T's door until she comes out into the hallway and sees what you did and grabs a handful of your hair and marches behind Ed-the-janitor, who scoops up the other kid and brings him to the nurse's office.

Ed-the-janitor leaves Mrs. T and the bleeding kid with a pair of scissors sticking out of his arm in the nurse's office and takes you by the arm to go see the principal. The whole way there, you stare at the blurry blue letters—USMC with an eagle, globe, and anchor—beneath the coat of fur on his forearm.

Sweat stings your eyeballs, and you blink, and blink, and blink, and the tattoo turns into a giant cross and the initials RT.

Dad's hands are clamped around your neck, cutting off the air, banging you against the back door in Grandma's kitchen. He's saying something, but it's getting hard to hear, and you're blinking your eyes slower now. Your fading consciousness convinces you it is the same as taking a deep breath. Something cats are said to do if they trust you. Your hands are clasped onto his wrists, but you are not fighting them as much as you are fighting gravity.

Grandma Audrey and Debbie scream at him to stop: *It was an accident It was an accident It was an accident.* But he keeps on until your back breaks through the wood of the panel door, and it separates from the hinge. Frustrated, Dad lets you fall to the floor like some filthy rag he can't believe he touched. It looks like he is out of breath as he grabs onto the doorframe with both hands, but then he stomps on your guts and nuts like he doesn't want you to live long enough to have any kids of your own.

This goes on until Grandma puts herself between the two of you and pushes him away. And surely there is more to tell, but when your brain is split between taking notes and shutting out the pain, you kind of turn out the lights and stare out the window, too.

YABBA DABBA DO

Commodities are not a raw material or primary agricultural product that can be bought and sold, such as copper or coffee. Commodities are why you stand in line at the community center on the first Saturday of every month. There you receive blocks of pasteurized cheddar cheese product that comes in the same sort of flimsy cardboard box the government uses for clips of M16 ammunition. You'd think your seven-year-old self could tell the difference between MREs and commodities, with those gallon tubs of peanut butter, boxes of instant nonfat dry milk, egg mix, seedless raisins, corn flakes cereal—all of which comes in nondescript white waxy cardboard packaging lined with aluminum, or something silver-colored. But then there are the rusted cans of carrots and green beans, along with the ones featuring the silhouettes of the animal supposedly inside:

BEEF with juices.

PORK with juices.

One Whole Chicken with Broth without Giblets.

There is bag after bag of sugar and flour, too. But being handed sticks of butter or tubs of margarine is not something there's a memory of. Neither is ever being out of Crisco.

If you're lucky, the local grocery stores pitch in boxes of macaroni and cheese. Not Kraft Macaroni & Cheese, but the kind that doesn't have a TV commercial.

Sometimes there is a twenty-pound sack of potatoes or a five-pound bag of apples. Sometimes they've already gone soft. There is always the bread that has to go straight into the freezer, so it won't go bad.

Let's not forget the farina: the flavorless, generic knockoff Cream of Wheat. Thankfully, there is always a big bowl of sugar on the table to fix its flavorlessness.

Grandma takes her coffee black—no sugar—so she doesn't care how much you put on your cereal, so there is always a little white crystallized island rising from the sea of milk in your cereal bowl. When the farina and fake corn flakes run out, there is a bowl of rice with milk and cinnamon to get you through until school serves something for lunch. The rice gets hard to eat after it turns cold. It's harder to eat once you see the kids you can help for just sixteen cents a day eating the same thing on the television set.

The Saturday after Halloween is when Grandma makes the first few batches of Christmas cookies. Thanks to her Betty Crocker cookbook looking like the collected works of Dickens, with dozens of dozens of recipes she's scissored out of the newspaper sticking out of the pages, half serving as bookmarks, you never know what she's going to make until it's time to lick the beaters or roll out the dough when she says her hands hurt.

Saturday morning is always one of solitude. It's when you wake to watch cartoons before the rest of the house stirs.

Friday night is when Grandma Audrey and Grandpa Bub spend the evening at the Moose Lodge doing their damnedest to outdrink one another, but that's after they go to the grocery store. It's almost winter, which means it's too cold to take you and leave you out in the parking lot with the dogs. But, because it's almost winter, it also means they can leave the food in the car and not worry about anything melting or defrosting in the back of the station wagon.

They put the bags where your feet go when you ride in the rear-facing seat. The metal floor keeps everything cold, and laying the rear-facing seat down flat turns it into something of a makeshift cooler.

But not bringing you with means Grandpa Bub will have to haul all the bags by himself. It also means you don't know what they bought, so the joy of finding a box of Fruity Pebbles in the Tupperware cabinet the next morning is nothing if not worthy of note.

It's not the generic stuff that kind of looks like Fruity Pebbles, the stuff that goes stale halfway through the bag despite Grandma putting it into a Tupperware pitcher. It's not *that* stuff you find, but Post Fruity Pebbles. Your favorite of all the cereals. Not the puffed rice cereal Grandma always gets, which is so bad the manufacturer doesn't even bother naming it. Not the stuff with the consistency of week-old popcorn, but Fruity fucking Pebbles.

Opening the cabinet and seeing the box is akin to discovering El Dorado.

You pour a bowl and drizzle ice-cold milk over the top, foregoing the spoonfuls of sugar. It is, after all, *wholesome, sweetened rice cereal*— it says so right there on the box—so you savor every spoonful until every orange, red, yellow, purple, green, and berry blue flake is gone.

The shitstorm that is the second grade fades away when the fruit-flavored tie-dyed milk splashes across the two thousand or so taste buds on your tongue. Chickadees sing their songs for you from their perches on the crabapple tree in the backyard while you drink down the last drop of milk.

It's that good.

When Grandma comes downstairs, you spring to your feet, ignoring the cartoons, not even waiting for a commercial break, and wrap your arms around her, hugging her, thanking her, reminding her how Fruity Pebbles is your all-time favorite.

Your words stop her patting the top of your head and cause her to march over to the Tupperware cabinet, where she sees you did indeed help yourself to a heaping bowl of Fruity Pebbles. Except they weren't for you and now she can't make her Christmas bars. But she still reaches for the rolling pin. Not the wooden one. The marble one. The one that has no other use than being ornamental, until the very second she uses it to crack your sacrum.

The doctor calls it a sacrum; everyone else calls it your tailbone. And Grandma tells the doctor it wouldn't have happened if you'd just slow down and walk down the stairs, rather than run.

PAPER OR PLASTIC

YOUR CHILDHOOD STINKS. MAINLY BECAUSE Grandma Audrey's house sits east of the paper mill, west of the sewage treatment plant, and two blocks north of a crematorium. There's nothing north of the neighborhood except the railroad tracks that bring in the trains filled with taconite pellets from the world's largest open-pit mine, which leaves the sodomized land with a gaping hole where the Misaabe-wajiw once stood. The only good thing that comes from all this is when the taconite pellets bounce out of the hopper cars and onto the tracks. They're like steel ball bearings the circumference of nickels and can take any window when launched from a wrist rocket.

It's a crapshoot as to what you'll be breathing while walking to the grocery store, which is now your main chore since the overstep with the Fruity Pebbles. Seeing as how you can only buy as much as you can carry, some days you get the full bouquet by the third or fourth trip back and forth, depending on which direction the wind is blowing.

The house is exactly three blocks from two different grocery stores. SUPERVALU to the west, which sits across the street from the high school, and Home Market to the east, which sits across the street from the elementary school. Home Market is basically a huge butcher shop. Most of what they sell comes by the pound or the slice. Other than that, they sell only a sprinkling of conveniences—never more than two or three of any one thing. Except for trading cards. You name it, they've got it: baseball, basketball, football, boxing, hockey, wrestling, Garbage

Pail Kids. But you only buy the ones that come with a complimentary piece of Bazooka bubblegum.

Nothing can ruin a day quite like a stick tumbling and shattering on the sidewalk. But on the other hand, when the white powder comes off the top card without it getting splattered with spit, there's next to nothing that can sour the afternoon.

Grandma sends you to pick up some bread and bologna one day, and for some reason, you decide to take a quarter and a couple of pennies from the leftover change to buy a pack of baseball cards—call it a shipping and handling fee.

Grandma counts the change against what the receipt says she should have, and she screams about how she's been robbed. She jumps out of her seat and says something about how she has to hide her jewels and runs up to her bedroom and stuffs the entirety of her jewelry box into her bra.

She doesn't hit you, though.

Instead, she chain-smokes and rocks in her chair at the dining room table and says she doesn't know what to do with you. It doesn't stop her from sending you shopping with a handful of coupons and a pocket full of cash, oddly enough. All the cashiers at SUPERVALU learn your face and notice when you come back to return an item.

When Grandma sends you to buy a bag of russet potatoes, you hang them from the handlebars and are too busy trying to get home lickety-split, like Grandma said, to notice the bag swings into the spokes when you turn a corner or pump the bike side to side to get going a little faster. The bag finally busts open about a half a block away from the house. The spokes hack off a half dozen or so potato chip–sized slices before a second potato slides from the bag, and you watch it take a turn around the wheel before it bashes into the forks and bends a few of spokes and sends you sliding across somebody's grass.

So much time has gone by that Dad stands on the front stoop looking for you, and when he sees you, he goes back inside and waits.

After you wipe your feet, he takes the bag away and slams your face into the front door for wasting Grandma's money. The second time he shoves your head into the door, you get the deadbolt smack dab in the side of the head. You don't even get to say sorry. Instead, you slump down to his feet and bleed onto the welcome mat.

While walking back to the kitchen, he notices you forgot the sour cream, too, and he lets the whole house know. When you don't bother to move, he takes hold of your two feet, plants his boot atop your bladder and ball sack with such force you can't help but piss your pants.

When you still don't get the hint to get up and go get the sour cream, he kicks you along the floor of the mudroom and down the steps of the stoop. You have to walk back to SUPERVALU and get the sour cream because you can't stand to sit on the seat or push through the pain to pedal the bike, wobbly as the front wheel is now.

LARGE PRINT

UNCLE HAROLD SQUINTS TO SEE who his visitor might be, smiling a curious, welcoming smile when the shadow crosses the threshold of his new room. He sits in the dark every afternoon so his roommate can nap, no matter who the roommate might be.

Navigating the room proves problematic until you see the neon orange vinyl chair glowing in the corner next to the bathroom door, beneath the television set. The same chair sits in the same spot in every room. This alone is enough to fill a fading memory with a bit of déjà vu.

An episode of *Matlock* projects an array of disorienting, shifting shadows—a kaleidoscope of blue and white hues—none of which help to illuminate the face of the silhouette taking a seat a few feet from the foot of the bed.

Uncle Harold sits and waits with sealed lips, quivering and clutching a dusty Bible.

The citrus-scented antiseptic spray stings your nose when you sit. It brings to mind the death and disease and bouquet of smells that come along with the last moments of life, the scent the staff work so hard to candy-coat. It's not like they're striving for some Good Housekeeping award. This is just the last stop before the funeral home. This isn't a retirement community plopped down amidst a Florida orange grove, but a hospice care facility in the shadow of an array of abandoned industrial monstrosities which once meant jobs but now whisper how Duluth is going the way of Detroit.

You slip off your coat, drape it over the arm of the chair, clutch a Bible too.

Uncle Harold releases the brake on his wheelchair and shuffles his feet, bringing himself closer to the neon orange vinyl chair an inch at a time. Seeing how long this is taking, you slide forward and lean into the light.

Surprises washes over him, makes his face fall, and he erupts into laughter, sounding something like a succession of hiccups. Genuine joy. A homing beacon from the years of your youth, along with Grandpa Bub's smoker's cough when you'd look up from the magazine rack and realize you were all alone.

This is Great-Uncle Harold, but that sounds weird. It sits too long on the tongue. He's Grandpa Bub's brother—not Dad's uncle—so, Great-Uncle Harold it is. To be technical.

"Oh, Jeff. It's good to see you. So good to see you." He leans forward, patting your knee countless times before squeezing it and taking a second to peer into your eyes.

"It's great to see you, too. New room, I see."

"Yah, got here after lunch today."

"How was it?"

"Gah…it's no good. Nothing like my Harriet ever made," he says, shaking his head, trailing off and doing what he can to swallow tears. "I can't believe she's passed," he continues, "Sandy too. They were good girls. Good girls."

You never know what to say when he brings this up. What do you say to someone who lost his wife and daughter in the same summer to the same cancer?

"That's a nice picture of you and Auntie," you say, pointing toward the dresser. "When was it taken?"

"Oh…at church. When they took portraits of all the members. Right before her first surgery. About two years ago now," he guesses, grabbing hold of the picture, wiping away the dust covering her face with a thumb, shaking all the while—not because of the ache in his heart, but because of the Parkinson's. "I kept some flowers from the visitation, but they haven't brought them over from my old room yet. Maybe tomorrow. You remind them on your way out, won'tcha, Jeff?"

You nod yes and clench your lips tight. It's painful to watch. Auntie Harriet has been gone for seven years. It's been eleven years since her first mastectomy. You'll buy some new flowers from the gift shop on the way out, as always.

He talks about missing his brothers, Eldon and Bub, before bringing up his sister-in-law, Auddie, as they called her. His face turns somber, and he clenches his teeth when he talks about how terrible she was to Bub and David. David especially.

"Oh, little Davey," he mutters, shaking his head in disgust. "And Bub was just as afraid of her. Mean old bitch," he whispers. He smirks and says, "Bub'd call me when she sent Davey to the grocery store, you know, and I'd make my way to SUPERVALU, quick as I could. We'd shop together, Davey and me. My little buddy. We'd get everything on Auddie's list, so he wouldn't get it when he got home. It was about a half a mile from Green Street. I sure miss the house, Jeff. How're the new neighbors? Are they keeping up my yard?"

He was always so proud of his lawn and his rose bushes. But Jeff you're not. You're David. This happens every time you visit. You can't recall the last time he remembered you.

The two of you went through this yesterday.

You take the time to answer his questions about his bushes and lawn in a way sure to make him smile. It might not hurt any for him to think you're Jeff, but you can't bring yourself to stay quiet. Maybe it's selfish, but you want to visit with Uncle Harold, which is why you fish your wallet from your coat pocket, slide your Military ID card out, tap it on his knee.

Like always, he takes it and holds it up to the light, and you watch while perplexity washes over his face. It breaks your heart, but you sit there while his smile fades. His subtle trembling turns to outright quaking accompanied by his eyebrows rising up as high as they can, seemingly lifting the corners of his mouth in an animated smile, smoothing out every wrinkle etched onto his face.

He stammers through your name, "Davey, Davey, Davey. Oh, Davey. Sergeant David! How about them apples," he says with a shaky yet crisp salute—beaming with pride.

"Say, there. How much bacon does a sergeant bring home these days?" he says, smiling so wide his lips barely move.

Your ballpark salary and housing allowance make him furrow his brow and bark, "You're not a goddamn Colonel!"

To put it in perspective, you tell him a newly-minted colonel makes ten grand a month.

"A month?" he repeats.

"A month," you echo back.

"Uncle Harold," you say, interrupting his whispered slurry of cuss words while tapping the Bible sitting on your lap. You peel the LARGE PRINT sticker off the cellophane wrapping. "Yesterday, you told me you couldn't read your Bible anymore."

"Ya—yesterday?"

"I thought you might like this," you say, and peel the cellophane wrapper away and place it on his lap.

Looking down, he opens the cover, taking note of the large print. A smile ripples across his face while shadows fall into the lines left around his eyes and the corners of his mouth by a life well-lived, but long forgotten. He flips through the pages, runs a finger beneath the lines of text. Then tears trail down the tip of his nose, and he begins a hymn not heard since you were Davey squished into the pew beside him and Auntie at Temple Baptist Church.

BEGGING THE QUESTION

THE DENTIST SENDS YOU TO the Navy headshrinker, so you stop dreaming, stop having nightmares, stop waking with broken bits of teeth on your pillow. Your sleeping problem curtails, but you never fully wake either. You walk around in a fog, drunk-like. It'd be fine if you didn't know you were in a fog. Lowering your guard is a different animal than having your guard lowered. They give you these pills and take your pistol, send you to bed early without dessert.

You'd rather court insomnia than be chemically impotent for a matinee viewing of a B-rated horror flick featuring special guest appearances by your most crippling fears. So you flush the bottle. See, these symptoms aren't symptoms over there; they're only symptoms when you're stateside, so you ask to redeploy.

It never enters your mind that you might make it home again.

Instead of your wife collecting life insurance, she files divorce papers. The thought of you being home day in and day out is too much to bear. Your commander knows your last ex-wife gets a quarter of your pay, and this one will get another quarter, and you'll only be getting half of what you were to begin with once they medically retire you, if you don't fight it.

The doctor says there's no way he will send you once more unto the breach. The commander argues, says you have adjustment disorder and the best place for you is being the harm in someone else's way.

The short version is they broke you, then send you out to stud.

Sending you out to stud looks a lot like you wearing a Barney Fife costume and checking IDs at the IT office of an oil firm following a spill in the Gulf. When the contract expires, a hardware store hires you to sell lumber, until a two-ton bundle of pressure-treated lumber slides from the tongs of an extended forklift and crashes down onto the floor in the aisle directly behind you. You go prone, call for a status report from your team. Training takes over, muscle memory, reptilian mindset, whatever bow you want to put on it.

A short time after, it's explained how they want to employ veterans—just not war veterans. Flashbacks among the treated lumber and associates screaming at imaginary friends is not something they advertise in their weekly flyer. Though they'd like it to stay between the two of you.

You run every day, beat a punching bag senseless, buy a Mossberg 500 shotgun—the one with the adjustable stock, pistol grip, and breaching barrel—a bolt-action .30-06, an SKS, Cx4 Storm, and a .40 caliber Beretta S&W pistol, run obstacle course races, collect medals for all your valiant efforts, prepare for a campaign that'll never come—keep yourself combat-ready.

Once this dawns on you, you take a seat in the waiting room of the newly expanded mental health wing at the Biloxi VA, which it turns out is just a bunch of temporary trailers bolted to one another. It's impossible to focus on any one thing because of this disjointed symphony of sound swirling around inside your ear canals. There is a game show TV host and his contestants, veterans from the last hundred years of war, all talking to each other and themselves. The psychiatrist has to call your name a handful of times and has a diagnosis ready before you finish crossing the waiting room. You have one eyebrow cocked in each direction and stare at her unblinking. She doesn't stop to think you can't hear what she is saying or that you're wondering why she is trying to speak over the crowd.

She doesn't close her door. She doesn't know if you're dangerous. But she knows you are dangerous, meaning: she knows you were sent to war, time and again, and made it back, time and again. But she doesn't know if you're a threat to her.

She has a hunch you're a danger to yourself.

There's no proverbial couch or reclining chair or ambient lighting in her office. There's only the metal folding chair she offers you and the ergonomic one she's sat down into. Now it's her who's unblinking. She asks, "Are you in immediate danger of hurting yourself?"

You tell her you wouldn't do that to your kids. You wouldn't put that stigma over them, which leads her questions concerning your family. You tell her your mom is dead, your stepdad is dead, your dad is—but she cuts you off and asks again about *your* family.

You don't want them to know you when you're like this. You'd rather die than explode on them for simply being kids. To have them fear you would kill you.

"You'd rather die?"

Yes, you explain. You'd rather die than have your kids afraid of you. You'd rather they not know you than fear you. You feared your father and hated him. He feared his father and hated him but stayed the course, wouldn't break with family tradition. Dad was able to articulate this feeling—this fear he felt for his father—yet he did the same to you, day in and day out. You may not be brain damaged like he is, but there is something wrong with you.

"One final question," she says. "What if you didn't have your kids? What would stop you from hurting yourself then?"

"The safety," you say in a measured whisper.

"Can you speak up, please?" she asks.

"Nothing," you say with a shrug. There'd be nothing to stop you if you didn't have kids.

She reads the symptoms someone has plugged into the computer following your first visit with the primary care physician and prescribes you something they're using to treat major depressive disorders, anxiety, and alcohol dependence. She warns of the side effects—shaking the bottle each time she shares something off the list: cottonmouth, fainting, vomiting, headaches, *more* frequent suicidal thoughts, unmasking and exacerbating an otherwise latent bipolarism, irregular heart rate, and priapism.

Priapism grabs your attention and causes an eyebrow to lift, letting her know it's not a word you know. She holds up her fist and unfurls her pointer finger, and you get her point.

You ask how often she'll need to see you.

"I won't," she says. "Either the pills will work or they won't. If they don't work, stop taking them. You can call, and we'll try something else."

You nod.

"Otherwise, call the pharmacy for a refill when they run out. And if things get really bad, call the crisis line."

You leave armed with a pocket full of pills and a refrigerator magnet.

MAYBE

Maybe your dreams and triggers are similar in more ways than you'd care to admit. Whether a trigger is real or a logical leap, the effect on the body is the same. Let's not forget how a dream is a dream, whether you label it a dream or a nightmare, and both are incomplete stories seeing as how they have no beginning or end.

There is the first part you can recall, but it's not the beginning.

It's more than likely you are subconsciously stuck in the middle of a nightmarish daydream with no end in sight. But that doesn't bother you once you remember an end to a story means the conclusion of a story. And who of sound mind looks forward to the end of their story?

Think of a snake bite. You'd remember the fangs piercing the flesh, but it would take a few precious seconds to register what took place, so the story begins after the snakebite happens. Unless, of course, you have the good fortune of watching it happen, or, if it's a rattlesnake and you hear the shake of the rattles, but there are still a few surprising nuances to the story of which you were unaware.

You've never experienced a poisonous snakebite, but you've been stung by eighty wasps at once, haven't you?

That may be an exaggeration.

They don't all sting you at the exact same time. They attack your face, neck, arms, not to mention your feet and ankles. The wasps work their way inside your shirt. Others travel up the insides of your pant legs. Others still make their way inside your tighty-whities, even after you cannonball off the dock and into Elliot Lake. They crawl along the skin and congregate in the pockets of air trapped underneath your clothes and continue to sting until they lose interest.

Glen somehow got you out of the lake and up to Grandma in the cabin. For the life of her, she couldn't figure out what was wrong with you. No matter how many times she asked, she was only answered by your hysterical interpretive dance. You cried incoherently and slapped yourself.

She'd thought you'd lost your marbles.

Most of the wasps were alive when she stripped you down to your birthday suit in the front room of the cabin. Peeling wet clothing off a kid who won't stop dancing and screaming is probably why medical professionals won't hesitate to produce a pair of trauma shears and just be done with it.

Once your shirt is up over your head, Grandma Audrey yells, "Bub, get me the witch hazel!" which he does before he goes around the cabin with the flyswatter killing every wasp he can find.

It's Grandma who counts the eighty bites. It's Glen who gets rid of the Super Soaker squirt gun you filled with ammonia, thinking it would kill the wasps that built their paper nest on the corner of the boathouse.

There's no telling how it began, or what made you weaponize a squirt gun, or how Glen let you pull the trigger on his Super Soaker and shoot a stream of ammonia into the nest, the stream they followed back to you, the source of the assault. Still, pain has a way of beginning a story off in a fog, and *maybe* becomes the mortar the other—known—details are stacked upon.

There are too many maybes that come before when Dad hammers his fist down on top of your skull, slamming your knees into the floor where the cabin meets the screened-in front porch. Your chest and face slap against the floor, too. You never saw it coming, so maybe Dad was standing behind you when he hit you.

You're told you stand up and say something like, "That didn't hurt," almost begging to get hit again, but he doesn't. He doesn't respond to your sarcasm. Instead, he lets you walk into the back bedroom and lie down on the bottom bunk. Or maybe someone says, "Go to your room," or maybe it's reflex by that point: you get hit, you go to your room. Or maybe when someone gets hit that hard they can't hear anything for a while. Either way, what you're told came after is Grandma screaming at Dad, saying something like, "Don't you ever touch *my* David again!" along with ordering him to leave her cabin. Before he does, Glen draws breath into his chest and bows up to Dad, not knowing what will come next. He wants to hit his Uncle Dickie, knowing he went too far and wanting him to remember that.

You wake inside a two-man raft, and when you peer over the side, you see velvet Elvis in his white jumpsuit hung on the wall at the foot of the bed. All you want to know is whether it's okay for you to come out of the bedroom and go to the outhouse. The cabin is quiet, and it's still daylight. Your bladder burns bad enough to make you brave enough to climb down to the floor, squeeze your nose and mouth outside the aluminum bifold door, and ask if you can go pee.

"Yes," Grandma says.

You tiptoe by her and Grandpa Bub, who is sitting in the corner, lunging back and forth in his rocker. He watches every step you take.

You know you're really in trouble when you see him standing at the door, staring at the outhouse. He watches you walk back to the cabin. He even opens the door for you to move things along a little quicker.

Grandma made a plate for you and sits watching while you eat. She burns through two cigarettes in the time it takes you to eat the two halves of the ham and cheese sandwich.

She doesn't give any word of warning, so you have no clue what is coming.

Three days came and went since Dad cracked you in the skull. Grandma wanted to take you to the hospital, but she was sure they'd take you away from her, or Dad to jail. Or both.

She knows she was a bad mother. But she got tired of bringing Dad to the bus stop and taking him downtown to his appointments at the Medical Arts building. She had to carry him. He was only six, but his three-quarter body cast made him so heavy, and she couldn't get the monstrosity of a wheelchair onto the bus. Nor could she stand people's stares. So she kept him home.

Anytime he'd act up or act out, she'd say, "Don't upset Richard" or "Don't make Richard mad."

It became her mantra.

People would mock her, repeating those words when she wasn't around. But back then, your kid was your business. Not that the help he needed existed in 1950. But when you came to live with her in 1980, she looked at him, and herself, and how she parented him, and how he turned out, and she'd be goddamned if she let you turn out the same way.

Though, that day at the cabin, she admitted there was something wrong with her Richard. He almost killed her David. And still, no one can say what you did to make him hammer his fist down on your head.

There's just a bunch of maybes.

I'M SORRY, SANTA

THIS IS WHAT HAPPENS WHEN you wake to the whirl of a hairdryer and wait to get your wits about you before you wander down the hallway to the toilet but realize Grandma Audrey is working the black corn silk atop her head into a perfect bouffant. You worry you might wet yourself if you try to wait her out again, so you pull on your Alf slippers and get ready for the three-story tiptoe to the manhole in the basement. Grandpa leaves it cracked open so he can take a leak whenever Grandma takes up residence in the bathroom.

You crack the bedroom door and see a plume of smoke from her Raleigh Lights fill the hallway, coupled by a cloud of Aqua Net, so you set your feet into a sprinter's stance and stand where she can't quite see you. Next is something of a waiting game, which you lose. She senses you being there and sticks her hand out, holding two squares of single-ply. Scrappy crapped in her closet again. Defeated, you take hold of the shit-paper and slog down to the opposite end of the hallway, where her bedroom awaits.

The floor shifts from your moving weight, and the door eases open, welcoming you inside. Once upon a time, this sent you running, convinced the house has a ghost.

You pause for a breath and nudge the door the rest of the way open, waltzing into a wall of Grandpa's Hai Karate aftershave. The bottle bakes in the morning sun, and the cracked cap fills the front room with a smell you know to be unnatural even at your tender age. You've learned to hide your nose and mouth inside your shirt when you make your way by her hamper, but it's of no use. The warm wafting smell of unwashed granny panties still reaches the back of your throat and sits on your tongue, taking away any hankering you had for breakfast.

You pause, blink, peer into the mouth of her closet and stall for a split second to let your eyes adjust, yet you know you need to get the job done before she comes to see what's taking so damn long. Still, when you step inside, your foot falls right into the dog shit, and your slipper smears the Lincoln Log starter kit–sized pile of Boston Terrier turds clear across the floor.

Tossing the toilet paper aside, your hand flails overhead in the hopes of finding the string. After hearing the metal end clink against the ceramic fixture, you wait for it to pendulum back toward the palm of your hand, which it does. With one yank, you've illuminated a preponderance of tiny metallic ribbons and bows splayed atop a pile of presents. They draw you toward the back of the closet, where you peel open each and every one of the to-from labels, leaving a trail of shitty footprints as you go.

Most of these gifts are emblazoned with your name. Some are meant for Debbie, but it's okay. She deserves something, right? Even with her being so old she's almost out of the house.

Satisfied with this bounty of gifts, you turn back toward the door to discover the mess you've made and absently slide off your slippers, sail down the steps, going faster and faster until you move faster than your legs can carry you and you plant your ass on the second to the last step.

Holding it in for so long makes you quiver from the searing pain and piss across the tops of your own two feet while standing astride the manhole in the bowels of the basement. Once the pressure lessens enough to allow you to breathe normally, the bouquet of smells in the basement evaporates the last of the early morning fog, and you remember you need to grab the mop and slink back upstairs and swab the floor clean, which you do. Mostly.

But you've missed a spot.

Shoving the hangers that hold her shirts and skirts to the side so you can wipe away the last little streak, you see another pile of boxes, all yet to be wrapped: Battle Cat, The Claw, Lite Brite, Construx, Photon, GI Joe and Micro Machines. Overjoyed, you spit a slurry of swear words and slap a hand over your mouth. If she knew what you'd found, you'd get socks and underwear instead for sure. Not to mention, she'd take up a handful of those clothes hangers and beat you into the middle of next week, again.

Christmas comes and the turkey gets carved, the cranberries uncanned, the carols are sung. The voices from the living room slur through all the standards while the excited voices of the grandkids crack and squeak, the whole pack sitting around the Christmas tree waiting for word that it's okay to tear into the gifts from Grandma and Grandpa. But the ritual bores even the jolliest of the cousins, and Bing Crosby gets switched out for the Chipmunks, then Ray Stevens, then the radio gets switched on, and all in attendance are treated to a medley of contemporary tunes, including the one you'll never forget the words to:

Grandma Got Run Over by a Reindeer.

Everyone sings along when it comes on. It's funny. It's about a grandma who's been drinking too much eggnog, who forgets her medication and walks home on a snowy Christmas Eve.

Tragically, she's found trampled to death the next morning.

Grandma Audrey bellows out to the house, "You'd all just love it if that was me, wouldn't you? You want me to up and die." The house is hauntingly quiet until Aunt Bobbie lets go a nervous laugh and says, "Oh—c'mon, Ma," and the needle is again run through Bing Crosby's Christmas classics.

For the youngest, you, it's bedtime. It's a stupid song anyway. Reindeer don't run down the street. They fly from rooftop to rooftop.

You close your eyes.

You open your eyes.

You stumble down the stairs bleary-eyed, see how one of the cookies is gone, the other only half eaten. *Wasteful.* "Finish it. There are starving children in Africa," Grandma would say to Santa. Meanwhile,

Tippy squishes her head into the cup, doing what she can to finish off the milk. Erring on the side of caution, you take the cup into the kitchen before she can knock it onto the carpet. She yowls when you take hold of the handle, which is why you don't dump it down the drain. You know she'd exact some sort of revenge for being robbed of this one simple pleasure. Instead, you pour what's left into her bowl.

You know what would happen if you tore into any of the wrapping paper before there is a camera to capture the magic of Christmas, so, instead, you spill the stocking out onto the floor and wait. And wait. You pull the Polaroid camera out of the bottom of the buffet and ready a new pack of film. Breakfast becomes a plastic candy cane chock full of Sixlets. The bundles of batteries and blank cassette tapes hint at what lies beneath the tree. Last year the fat man forgot the batteries. Things are looking up.

Then hunger strikes again.

Brunch becomes a slice of cornflake Christmas wreath atop a bowl of peppermint ice cream—recompense for having to sit staring at Christmas gifts for hours on end.

When the sun comes up, you turn the television on with the volume down as far as you can, and you wait some more.

You try the trick with the coffee pot taught to you by Folgers' commercials, but they still do not wake. The coffee burns long before you hear the click and creak of their bedroom door.

Her hellhounds need tending before anyone is allowed to open a single gift, so you ready their water dish and pour their kibble while the rest of the household trickles down the stairs. Then, like Easter morning, you go on the hunt. It's your job to scurry about the house searching for their shit piles while Debbie drags gifts from beneath the tree.

Once the crap is cleaned up, you're able to take a seat at the edge of the couch by Grandpa's feet. You know which of the gifts you'll open first. You spent a good bit of the night tracing the packages through the wrapping paper, lifting them high overhead, and shaking them while listening for movement from the floor above.

The first box is a big one. Lite Brite. You push the box to the side and move on to the next one—after pausing for a picture, that is. Next, you peel back the paper and read the word *Photon* scrawled across the packaging. This slows you down, makes you look around the room. Maybe there was a mix-up. You told Santa you wanted Lazer Tag. Grandma must have bought this for Glen or one of the other grandkids. Then there's a dozen Micro Machines you unwrap, none of which will work on the Hot Wheels track you got last Christmas. Slick as you can, you go into the trash bag searching for the wrapping paper, which once adorned the presents. The tags are undeniable. There's no mix-up. You see Santa's name written in the scrolling cursive that comes just once a year.

All these presents came from the back shelf in Grandma's closet. This realization forces a smile to spread across your lips for fear of being asked, "What's wrong?" and having to admit you saw all these gifts before they were wrapped.

The next one to slide from the pile is obvious. Santa, somebody, whoever, did not even try to conceal what it is: an action figure. GI Joe. Spirit Iron-Knife and his pet bald eagle, Freedom. But it didn't come from Santa. It came from the closet.

A shovel topped with a bow sits propped up in the corner behind the tree, and the flakes are falling outside. But the doorbell rings and some other distant relative appears from the haze of Christmas past. You recognize her, but that's about it. Grandma greets her with a name you've only heard spoken a time or two—always in a venomous voice. She sits at the table and watches while you stuff the last of the wrapping paper into the trash bags. Then it's time to lug all the presents upstairs and change clothes, so you can leave with the little redheaded lady a little later.

The two of you ride in silence until she asks how you like the presents. You let her know you know about Santa, that Grandma Audrey signed Santa's name for him.

But she wants to know about the ones she dropped off for your birthday, back in October, and Christmas too. She brought things from her mother, your uncles, aunts, and cousins. At least a dozen gifts.

You're confused.

So you sit and listen to your mother rattle off a list of everything you asked for, and then some—including some things you'd never bother to ask for because you knew circling it in the Sunday morning ads would make Grandma say, "Don't be stupid," and "You're never happy with what I can give you."

But it was Mom who got you everything you thought came from Grandma Audrey and Grandpa Bub and Dad, as well as the fat man and his eight tiny reindeer.

GROUNDHOG DAY

MORNINGS ARE SPENT SCROLLING THROUGH social media: liking, sharing, so on and so forth—letting people know you're still breathing. Roll call complete. Twenty-two brothers and sisters die every day. None last night, though. You're still here, too.

For now.

Next is the morning news hour. Local first, then national, followed by more coffee.

Maybe breakfast.

A talking head tells you about a tragedy in Paris and what they know so far and how they think it can be avoided in the future. The president follows with his thoughts on what steps to take next. You laugh at all this—not because of its comedic value, but because you spent nine months watching over Class Charlie detainees: the worst Iraqis, Third Country Nationals, and former regime officials ever rounded up. Then you watch while a change in your own country's regime brings about the release of twenty-some-odd thousand of them back into polite society. One of which becomes a trainee of your unit while guarding the oil rigs in the gulf. You've no wonder where this new group found recruits.

This is why you'll stop watching television.

The news of attacks starring those with their faces hidden behind a shemagh churns up all you've worked to forget. Everything is breaking news now, so it all becomes background noise, but more like a mosquito buzzing right outside of arm's reach. The faceless enemy they love to flash across the television screen and tell you to hate is not the one you fear, though; they had their chance to bring you harm and failed. The man in the fogged-over mirror following your morning shit-shower-shave routine is who you can no longer trust not to hurt you or your loved ones.

The residents of your theater internment facility transferred to Camp Bucca, a prison made of canvas tents and razor wire with floors made of desert sand, where juvenile delinquents will slather themselves with their own shit to avoid being raped. And the American people wonder out loud why so many were radicalized in the encampments meant to keep them safe, warm, and fed until the time of their trial.

You'll get a fish tank. Then a bigger fish tank. Then an even bigger tank—big enough to violate your lease. The thing about fish growing to the size of their environment isn't entirely true. The Fantail grows to the size of a softball. The Shubunkin grows as long as your hand and forearm combined. The thing cannot even turn around in the tank anymore without bumping the glass. Watching them swim is supposed to be soothing, but it's depressing. It's worse than watching animals pace at the zoo, and you're the zookeeper.

It takes years to notice the series of prisons that structure this story. Every prisoner, conscious of their confinement, wants to escape. This thought becomes intrusive, then a source of mental decay. These thoughts are not a way to shirk off boredom or pass the time. They're what happens when demons are exercised, rather than exorcised— when they take you by both shoulders, shove you into a chair, and you don't offer a fight.

Instead, you sit slumped with a Beretta on your lap, mull over life's greatest hits and a few B-sides, thinking about what you've done.

Right then is when Mom's voice rolls in from the other room, breaks your concentration, really fucks up your derailing train of thought.

You blink, but don't budge.

She says your name a second time, but not your full name the way mothers do when their children have genuinely disappointed them—

she only says, "David." Though there's a tremble in her voice you've never heard before. It's a lot like when someone screams, and someone else takes to whispering, which makes the whispered words seem more frantic than the scream. Your eyes trace the shadows along the edges of the hardwood toward the carpeted floor of the bedroom where she's standing, hands on her hips, the way she does when she's discovered you still haven't done what she asked.

Ten years have passed since she passed, and you'd like nothing more than to see her face, but that's too bad; she's silhouetted by the streetlights outside the windows. Then, as if on cue, a set of turning headlights flood the room that cause you to lean forward in the hopes of getting your wish.

The Beretta falls to the floor.

The sound draws your attention away from her and to your feet. The gun doesn't go off, and she's satisfied that her special guest appearance is enough to reroute your deliberation and leaves you by your lonesome.

Out of sight, out of mind.

The phone rarely rings. The last time someone you knew called it was Mom's brother, Brian, on Groundhog Day 2005. He'd gathered the family first, gave them the news, then locked himself in his bedroom and gave you a ring, but got told to leave a message after the beep.

You're manning an entry control point on a Navy base in Mississippi when you notice the screen on your phone is aglow and says you have a missed call, so you tell the overwatch you need to hit the head and check a message.

The voicemail asks you to give your uncle a call back. You know what's coming: Grandpa Bill, Grandma Lynn's second husband, is on life support in a hospital in Phoenix.

Or was.

When Uncle Brian answers, you hear the house bustling around him like when you call at Christmas. But instead of passing the phone around to other family members, you hear him close himself on the other side of a door and ask, "Have you heard?"

"Grandpa Bill," you say more than ask.

"No, David, your mom."

"What? What's wrong with her?"

"She died."

"What? When?"

"Today."

The rest of the conversation isn't clear, or staticky, and you're unwilling to wrap quotation marks around it. One of you eventually has to hang up the phone, and then you'll slide down to the floor where you'll unsnap your pistol belt from around your waist and kick it as far away as you can. The bathroom door never latched quite right, so the overwatch catches a glimpse of you sitting on the floor, and asks, "What's wrong?"

"Call the watch commander."

He asks, "What's going on?" when he sees you with your phone in one hand and the pistol grip in the other. You're not thinking *suicide*, you're thinking *foul play*. You're thinking you can make it to Mom's apartment before morning, but you're not thinking straight. You've gone from a stoic sentry to a puddle. They see the have-gun-will-travel in your eyes and take away your car keys, and you write the inscription for Mom's headstone on a cocktail napkin on an airplane early the next morning.

You'll be fine if you can keep the pen moving.

Mom was the only one who encouraged you to write. She bought you a typewriter and then an electronic word processor, but the first thing you ever published is her obituary.

You write her eulogy at a tire shop right before you meet the reverend who suffers from Bell's palsy, and all you keep thinking is how he's going to slur and stammer the whole way through her final salutation. She deserves better, but this is all the family can afford.

Mom would slap you if she ever heard you say something of the sort. No, she'd give you nipple twisters. She knows you've been hit enough in this lifetime, so the one time you do bow up to her, remind her how much bigger than her you are, she reaches out and grabs onto your nipples, twisting them—up and out—making you even taller, sending you up onto your tippy-toes before setting you down onto your knees, and tells you you'll never be as tough as she is.

She was found cold on the bathroom floor, her husband tells you, still wearing her bathrobe from earlier that morning, from when he went to work.

These are details you didn't need, didn't want, will never shake.

You spent Mother's Day weekend at the Minneapolis MEPS a month before high school graduation. It would have—could have—should have—been the last Mother's Day you spent with her before you went away.

The first time you raised your right hand, your tattoos could still be counted. Six. Now a heart with *Mom* and her birthday followed by Groundhog Day 2005 is inked deep into the flesh of your forearm, but it's always covered by long-sleeved shirts. You think it'll soften your exterior and let the past fade into memory. You've tossed away your razors too—hoping it'll hide the clean-cut exterior so synonymous with the military man. But you still march with a thirty-inch step when you walk, swing your arms nine inches to the front and six to the rear, don't you? You still punctuate sentences with sir and ma'am, don't you?

You can still make *yessir* and *yes ma'am* sound a whole lot like *fuck you.*

The one letter you do receive while playing in the sandbox is from a high school somewhere in the Rockies. It's from a Support Our Troops school project, but this seventeen-year-old has other things in mind. The words in her letter allude to it, and the picture she slips inside, wearing what some might call a swimsuit, solidifies it.

The letter gets filed in the trash, but somebody fishes it out and tapes her picture to the back of one of the stalls in the bathroom. You sit in the dark, staring at it until your legs fall asleep, more times than you can count, wanting nothing more than a moment of silence, privacy, solitude. If you could lean forward far enough to prop your forehead against the stall door, you could finally get some rest.

You shit shower-shave in a bathroom big enough for a handful of men. Yet every morning, there is a handful crowded around each sink.

Some mornings you piss in the shower while shaving without the water running. A Hollywood shower will get your ass kicked. A quick rinse will do. If you even decide to turn the water on, that is. Last you heard, the water they truck in is tainted. Some Lieuy went home with E. coli, another with Hep C, so you rinse your feet off with the rest of the bottled water you brushed your teeth with, and you go about the day.

You'll be soaked with sweat soon enough anyhow, and once the sweat mixes with the kerosene the Kurds use to disinfect your uniforms, you'll be as headachy as you were the morning you left for boot camp—when you took down a case of Reddi-wip because you knew whippets wouldn't show up on a piss test. It's harmless, as is everything else when you're eighteen. It's never brought up while talking to the doc, unlike the black mold that wormed six inches deep into the concrete walls of the berthing at FOB Suse.

The mold is entered into everyone's medical record, so they have you take hold of this tube every now and again and blow and blow and blow and blow until it seems you'll black out. But you're no big bad wolf, and every year after Iraq, another thirty seconds gets added onto your runtime. The chief says you're getting slow, getting old. But then it's a medical retirement. And the all-for-one-and-one-for-all brotherhood is gone.

The VA asks about nonprescription drug use, and you flash back to finding mushrooms growing out of the top of some cow shit. Your partner says he thinks those are the magical kind, so you call Dispatch and tell them to go to a private channel and ask them to look it up on the internet, and, sure as shit, they are the magical kind.

The next thing you know, the two of you are shoveling the cow patties into the bed of the six-pack pickup truck—on the watch commander's orders—to dispose of them properly.

When you pull into Camp Garcia, the watch commander has mustered everyone who's marooned on the island with you for the next two weeks. He's fully acclimated to island life, as illustrated by his Speedo, combat flip-flops, pistol belt, and Oakleys.

He tells everyone they're looking at hallucinogenic mushrooms.

This is his impromptu drug identification course. Then he punctuates this by saying if one of us tries them, we all have to try them. Then he hollers for someone to go get the pizza pan, and he pulls the mushrooms off the patties with his Gerber one by one.

For some reason, your mind drifts back to winding your way barefoot through the neighboring farmer's field wearing nothing but a pair of tighty-whities and the bell Mom tied around your back and between your shoulder blades, because you have a habit of walking like a cat and sneaking off to wherever you so please, but, luckily, you were herded by the farmer's Australian Cattle Dog, Rocky. Rocky is growling at you, and Cici is growling at Rocky for growling at you. Cici doesn't like the farmer's son, so he can't get near you, let alone bring you back to the trailer, so he sets a can of Coke down on a tree stump and then goes to find your mom, who sees you sitting on a stump, sipping a Coke, kicking at Rocky. She asks, "What're you doing?"

"Dumb dog won't let me go see moo-cows!"

The farmer's kid turns Mom's attention toward the bull they brought in to breed with the heifers, standing less than fifty feet away.

DRIVE ON

You yank the wheel, forcing the front end of the vehicle to lunge from one lane into the next each time you travel beneath a bridge or underpass. Seeing someone standing atop an overpass quickens your pulse, dampens your skin, clamps fingers around your windpipe. Even when it's only a state trooper running radar. That's when you flashback to haji holding a sat phone, calling in your convoy's location and direction of travel. You blink your eyes a bunch, focusing on something new each time your eyelids flash open in order to ground yourself in the here and now, but you still call out objects along the route, "Stalled vehicle, left shoulder," and swerve to the far right. Rumble strips remind you of your place and time right up until a pile of trash bags left by those who adopted this stretch of highway thrusts your mind back into evasive maneuvers. Cones squeeze three lanes down to one. Traffic slows to a crawl, causing you to clench the steering wheel so tight your knuckles turn white and pop as violently as the last handful of corn kernels at the bottom of the microwave bag while the rest blacken and burn.

But you'll buckle up and do it again the next day, every day, Monday through Friday. Your mind drifts while behind the wheel, wondering whether the ninety-day bottle of blood pressure pills the VA prescribed could slow your pulse enough for it to cease until an oncoming car issues out of the ether, which is enough to jumpstart your heart and force your head out of your ass. So you rattle your head, hoping to force blood back between your ears, but all you manage to do is send your glasses sliding to the tip of your nose.

Put your hands at ten and two then slide them down to five and seven because of the thing about the airbags breaking wrists, etc. Try to look professional, at least, for when the oncoming traffic gets close enough to see you behind the wheel.

Keep in mind the weather is overcast, meaning: everything is grayscale. Neither the sun, sky, or clouds will reflect in the glass and turn the windshields opaque.

This other driver, her hands are at one and eleven. She's hunched forward in her seat, peering over the top of the wheel with her eyes fixed on the road ahead of her. When you see those big square glasses with the rounded corners and that pixie-cut red hair glittering with little specks of salt and pepper, like you haven't in some ten-odd years, you forget to allow breath into your chest. Her gaze doesn't leave the road. She looks petrified. It's the expression Mom has plastered on her face every time she needs to get somewhere in a hurry, especially when one of her kids needs her.

Another time, while merging from the highway onto the freeway behind a big rig, someone in the slow lane doesn't see you or the truck until it's too late and sideswipes the car next to them in the passing lane, sending them into the concrete divider. It's a safe bet the slow driver didn't see them either. You hear warm rubber squeal against oily tarmac along with an implosive crunch of collapsing aluminum and steel. You cast your eyes to your driver's side mirror in time to see a sedan ricochet, overcorrect, come barreling toward you.

The car comes so close it disappears from the rearview mirror before it bends the guardrail right behind your rear quarter panel and in full view of the passenger side mirror.

It lifts off the freeway.

The grille, windshield, bumper cover all explode into the air, into fragments, shards, shrapnel. The fenders bend and crease. The hood releases and raises, blocks the view of those inside, so you can't see their faces as you speed away from the raining debris that resembled an automobile a few seconds earlier.

You floor it, push through, and don't let up until the big rig disappears from the rearview mirror—almost missing your exit in doing so.

You complete the stop at the next lab robotically, replete with beeps and boops courtesy of your scanner, and take a shortcut through Grandma Audrey's old neighborhood on the way to the next clinic before heading back downtown to the main testing lab at the hospital. Her house is hidden behind a row of saplings planted by the new owners right after they moved in, right after Grandpa Bub passed—less than a year after Grandma died of a stroke while withering away from cancer. The trees are towering now, taller than the highest peak of the roof. The front stoop has fallen away from the foundation and sunk down into the dirt. The garage leans against the neighbor's now. Grandma's rose bushes no longer perforate the front yard from the neighbor's. Instead, a six-foot-tall trellis stands in their place. Children play beneath the boughs of the tree where you once danced a jig at the end of an enormous dish towel, before it ripped and tore and plopped you down into the dirt. The rest of the house hides behind the neighbor's hedges, no matter how slow you ease through the intersection.

You don't want to go straight home after you punch out. It's been the kind of day when you'll lie on the couch and stare at the ceiling until the next morning, when it's time to go do it all again. So you take the scenic route and grab groceries for the next week before you head to where the pets go and grab Bentley a bag of food. Though that doesn't turn out to be as mindless and distracting as you'd hoped.

You stop dead in your tracks at the edge of the parking lot. This place sends you back to high school, when Mom worked here—washing dogs and expressing anal glands, trimming toenails, beautifying a goat or two. You'd take the city bus up here after school and wait for her shift to end, so you didn't have to take the school bus home.

It's been more than ten years since her cremation, yet here she sits, beneath the bus stop with her back scooted up against the wall. Every memory, every photograph, every conversation you had with her flips through your mind the way a possessed slide projector does, disorienting the unsuspecting protagonists in a horror movie. It's as if every image you have of her is trying to show itself to you at the same time to make sure you understand this is Mom.

She's dressed like her.

Her hair is cut like her.

Her voice sounds like her.

But she hasn't aged a day.

You can't put what she's saying in quotation marks because of the passing cars and the excitable conversations of families with their new puppies and their yappy little kick-me dogs. But it's her voice. You know her laugh, and you've heard her grumble and yell and mutter and slur enough to know her voice when you hear it. And you are hearing it.

When you dare walk closer, you see she's not well. She's talking to herself about the nonsensical. You've carried Mom home from the bar and heard her talk like this more than once. She's laughing to herself and looking toward the sky and looking at things passing on the sidewalk that no one but she can see. You laugh at yourself a little, too, and chalk it up to how you've stumbled upon a person affected with autism, maybe, or someone who's away from their group home and is in sensory overload, or someone who has simply missed their meds. But when the automatic doors part, she makes a guttural utterance and you look her way in time to catch her in a moment of clarity.

She stares into your eyes, looks at you the way Mom did when she knew you did something wrong, she just didn't know what yet. But she'd figure it out soon enough.

People have to walk around you so they can get inside.

She keeps giving you this look and giving you this look, and you know this look, and you know those eyes. You can close your eyes and see her face any time you want, but she's sitting on the ground right in front of you, here and now, waiting for the bus.

The same bus you took to come and see her.

When that thought enters your mind, she shoots you another look, the one that tells you she knows you're up to something and you better stop it—right now. There's nothing to do but hang your head, shove your hands into your pockets, and walk through the glass doors.

You don't know what else to do but let this marinate.

In your right pocket, you feel a set of car keys. In your left pocket, you feel the pills you should have taken three hours ago with the lunch you never got to eat.

THE LAST DANCE

YOU KNOW THE DANCE PEOPLE do when they're trying to pass one another, the left-right-left-right-right-left dance, when the two of you are trying to figure out who's leading and who's following?

The last time you do that dance with Grandma Audrey is right before Easter dinner, during the spring of the sixth grade. You're in the doorway between the dining room and the kitchen when she lambastes you and yells, "Get out of my goddamn way!"

You don't blink. You look down. You have to now if you mean to look her in the eyes. "Why are you hitting me?" you say, shaking your head. "It doesn't hurt anymore."

Grandma's eyes flash, and her ears flush, and she favors her hand. You let her know you've taken note of the last little bit, nodding toward her hand, saying, "It hurts you more than it hurts me."

The only sound in the room while you walk out to the kitchen is Auntie Harriet's sobbing on the far side of the dining room table. Through tears, you hear Auntie say, "Leave him alone, Auddie, he's numb. He's numb now."

Grandma Audrey grabs hold of the metal-edged yardstick she keeps tucked between the bookcase and the wall that separates the kitchen and the dining room. Seeing this, you walk to the back of the kitchen, out of sight for everyone sitting silently in the dining room except Auntie Harriet, who continues to cry.

Grandma follows on your heels but freezes in her tracks when she watches you push the button on the microwave for a ten-minute-long defrost cycle.

You don't say anything. You fold your arms across your chest and watch her pace.

There's a box she wears on a belt that's attached to a pair of electrodes that monitor her heart. The box is sensitive to microwaves, and Grandma has it in her head if she gets too close the box will stop working, and so will her heart. No one corrects her misunderstanding.

This is how you put Grandma in time out, give her time to think about what she's done.

This is how you parent.

SUICIDE CHECKERS

FAMILY IS MUCH EASIER TO keep straight if you remember it this way:

Grandma Audrey's and Auntie Harriet's first husbands were both named Gene.

Their second husbands were brothers: Grandpa Bub and Uncle Harold.

Grandpa Bullshit is twelve years older than Grandma Lynn.

Grandma Lynn is twelve years older than Dad.

Dad is twelve years older than Mom.

Mom is twelve years older than Debbie.

Sam is three years and two months older than you.

You are three years and two months older than your little sister.

Your great-uncle's twin was stillborn.

Your uncle's twin was stillborn.

Your twin was stillborn.

Your father is five when he gets hit by a car.

Your nephew is ten when he and his bike bounce off the windshield of a moving automobile, leaving him thinking he's in trouble for hurting the car.

You are fifteen when a '77 Caprice Classic sends you spinning headfirst into a giant concrete planter, leaving you with yet another concussion, along with a cracked sinus cavity, seventeen breaks on your lower leg between the knee and ankle, and a shattered wrist.

Dad married three times.

Mom's fourth husband finds her dead on the bathroom floor.

Maybe you'll beat them both with a fifth time to the altar. It's a game of numbers, like checkers—three rows of four, twelve in total. Dad teaches you how to play. He doesn't sit you down and read you the rules. He can't. He can't even read your birthday cards aloud without embarrassing himself, so he teaches you the same way he teaches every other lesson learned: he waits until you fuck something up or it looks like you're going to beat him at his own game.

It's his game, after all.

He keeps the black and red checkerboard folded up inside the drawer of the end table between the two recliners, along with the two dozen checkers, discs that are sometimes called men, black and white men.

Dad is always black, he always goes first. You're always white, you always go last. Along with those men in the drawer is a loaded pistol, a Mexican switchblade, a handful of guitar picks, and about a half-dozen condoms that look older than you. He even goes so far as to tell you which one he almost used the night he first slept with Mom. You cut him off, telling him you don't want to know, it's something a child should never know. But he must have worn one, after all. He calls you Ripped Condom—like it's your Indian name.

So, checkers. Dad sets up the bifold cardboard checkerboard on a TV tray so that there is a black square on the bottom left-hand corner for the both of you. He puts his black men on his black squares, and you set the white men on your black squares. He says, "You can move the men forward one space diagonally, in either direction, to an open black square, but the red spaces are off-limits. It's like the reservation: no place for white guys or niggers. A man can only move forward and can't land on a square that's already taken."

When you jump a guy, you get to take him off the board. This continues until all your guys are gone, and Dad wins.

He explains this as he goes along, saying things like, "Nope, put it back."

He wins every time.

The rules say you should switch men after every game, but Dad won't ever touch the white checkers unless he's stacking them up along his side of the board—the white men he's taken out. The rules also state if you've made every move you can, and you can't move anymore, if the pieces are locked or blocked, then you've won.

This is called Suicide Checkers.

Telling Dad you've won is just asking for a beating. It's suicide.

If you do win, then you've obviously cheated, and Dad doesn't want to play anymore.

He'll put the men and the board back in the drawer without saying a word, other than, "Get me a beer." And sometimes, while you're busy, he'll grab a flat pick out of the drawer and strum his guitar for a song or two. Sometimes he'll play "Dueling Banjos," all by himself, without missing a note. He'll fade from that song right into some Flamenco guitar music. You'll sit on the footstool and watch, mesmerized by this man and the sounds coming from the hollow body of his 1955 Dove acoustic guitar.

HOMECOMING

"THE DAY YOU CAN TAKE me is the day you can move out," Dad lets go with a grunt, hoisting himself up out of the driver's seat.

You say nothing.

You quietly collect your bags out of the back seat and listen to his cowboy boots clomping against the pavement on their way toward the back door of his concrete cube of a house. You make sure to move slow enough for his footfalls to turn into a fading echo, and you wait for him to say something about molasses in January, but you're met by silence. The tacet ends when the storm door spring screams, letting you know he's standing in the darkened foyer fumbling with his keys.

You take your time gathering the handles of the bags in your hands. You don't dare enter until the deadbolt tumbles open. History tells you how he'll wind up backhanding you if he's delayed in any way—for blocking his light, most likely. Not to mention, it's warm out, and Dad is a stout, sweaty man who smells of stale cigarette smoke, cheap beer, baby powder, and eye-stinging cologne that comes in a ridiculous-looking decanter, along with a subtle hint of the piss he couldn't be bothered to shake off. The back porch hallway is lined with plastic Kmart bags filled with crushed beer cans that he vows to take to the recycling center. Stale beer pools at the bottom of each bag and trickles down onto the floor, causing the whole mess to cling to the tile floor in one solid, fused mass, as if a mush-mouthed Moses worked as a barback.

Light glints through the crack where the porch pulls away from the house, allowing ants and flies and hornets and all sorts of winged things to congregate in, on, atop the bags. They get drunk on the skunky, syrupy brew and forget about stinging or biting you. But God help you if one comes into his house when you open the door.

The reason for all the keys is a simple one: ever since the judge ordered Dad to pay child support, he's worked on a barter system of sorts.

Everything with him is under the table.

One of his drinking buddies, Roger, owns AMO Automotive, an auto repair shop that's mingled amongst a liquor store, a pawnshop, an adult bookstore/peep show, a bathhouse, and an abortion clinic—you know, historic downtown Duluth. At the shop, Dad welds whatever is needed. In return, he's given free rein to use the shop's tools, as well as access to Roger's expertise whenever whatever is ailing the Reliant's engine proves beyond Dad's mechanical understanding. Sometimes you get free entertainment, when his sweaty hands slip from the slick chrome handles and smash into sharp, greasy pieces of metal under the hood.

He comes and goes from Roger's shop when he pleases. That's where one set of the keys come from. It's not as if he punches a time clock. Mostly, he loiters there throughout the day and drinks cup of coffee after cup of coffee. You too find employment there. Dad won't let another man teach you about cars, but you're allowed to push a broom around the shop and take out the trash once school is done for the day.

If you don't have detention, that is.

You tell Dad it's track practice, but it's detention. When you don't have detention, and Dad's not home, and the fridge is little more than beer and A1, ketchup and Miracle Whip, or a bag of frozen French fries and a brand-new box of Banquet chicken in the freezer, which you don't dare touch, you take the bus downtown to where you're given the key to the vending machines in exchange for some end-of-the-day janitorial work.

Once the bus crosses from the west side of downtown to the east, you ding the bell to let the driver know you want off. You have to make your way past the pro-life protesters and take a left once you see the bongs and dildos in the windows of The Last Place on Earth, never lifting your head until you come to the alley after the Family Sauna, which is a little different than the Yoshiko Sauna, which is where grown men go to get a backrub and jerked off by thirteen-year-old Chinese girls. The Family Sauna is where family men go to be homos before they go home to their wives, according to Dad.

Some days you do dumb shit, like pop the oversized bubble wrap the engine parts come in while Roger adjusts the timing on some foreign job. He sends you to the public library for a Chilton book, so he can figure out what the fuck is wrong with the imported piece of shit, his words, but once you break the rhythm of the popping, Roger stops looking at the engine and searches around the garage and sees what you're doing and sends a pair of channel locks sailing toward your head.

"Knock it the fuck off," he says.

So you take the trash downstairs and out back to the dumpster in the alley. Before you head back upstairs, you head to the bathroom and beat your meat to the pair of tits hanging over the toilet tank courtesy of this month's *Easyrider* centerfold. But first, you make sure to wash your hands. You lather up with two full pumps of the Gojo natural orange pumice hand cleaner—a combination of baby oil, scrubbing particles, and citrus scent—which moisturizes the skin and leaves your hands softer than any girl you've ever met.

Another set of keys belongs to the bar where Dad works. He wakes you and takes you to the bar after closing time. Sometimes the two of you arrive in time to see the owner closing out the register before heading up the stairs to the apartment above. Dad and the bar owner always exchange pleasantries. They share the same first name. They are both Dick(s).

Dad calls the bar owner *Little Dick* because he looks so skinny it seems like he lives off caffeine, cigarettes, and lite beer. The bar owner calls Dad *Big Dick* because he tips the scales at two hundred and fifty-plus pounds. They even have their nicknames embroidered on the front of their dart league jackets. Together they look like Laurel and Hardy if the fat one was Indian.

You sit at the bar with a Dr. Pepper and nibble away on Harvest Cheddar Sun Chips, staring at yourself in the gold-flecked mirror while Dad sweeps the whole place down and cleans the tabletops with a rag which is anything but.

Sometimes you fall asleep with your forehead resting on the bar, and Dad will wake you, saying, "Hey, ya lush, go find a booth to lie down on until I'm done."

Before you nod off again, you watch him wipe down the entirety of the dining room, mop every inch of the floor. He's methodical. One by one, he sets the dining room chairs atop the tables, counter-clockwise. He does the same with the barstools, spinning them until they sit aligned with one another in a perfect row.

In the kitchen, he cleans the bar glasses, then the grease traps, followed by the rubber floor mats, all of which are sent through a monstrosity of a dishwasher that belches a cloud of steam each time Dad opens the side door. The cloud billows out into the barroom, leaving a sheen of moisture on every surface.

It's said you sleep like a cement truck. You slide off the vinyl bench seat onto the floor and stink of Simple Green well into the next afternoon.

For years you had it in your head how Dad brought you along to show you how you'd need to put your all into whatever you do, even if it is nothing more than cleaning up a tavern come closing time. But that's not the case. Later, you learn how he didn't do it to put food on the table or keep the lights turned on, or to make sure you stay warm in the winter, either. No, in exchange for services rendered, he's allowed to drink all he wants during their regular business hours. It's how he pays his tab, in other words. There's no lesson about grit and spit and elbow grease or a hard day's work here. Dad most likely brings you along because he doesn't dare leave you behind, in fear of Grandma learning he left you by yourself when he took you for the weekend, so the two of you could do whatever fathers and sons do when killing time together.

It helps him do more than keep an eye on you. If the food stamps run out, he can make you something to eat for dinner before he dumps the deep fryer grease. If you can call it dinner at two in the morning, that is.

The inside of Dad's house is sad. The kitchen table is barely visible beneath a collage of empty Banquet chicken boxes, microwave TV dinner trays, beer cans and bottles. Styrofoam meat trays still stuck to their blood-soaked pads sit in a stack on the edge of the stove. Some harbor green bits of mold. The more recent are decorated with tiny craters from being pelted with scalding-hot grease—a result of him cooking at far too high a temp or being far too drunk to bother looking for a lid, which is impressive considering how many memories you can call to mind of him swaying in a figure-eight while bellied up to the stove, shirtless, fixing something to eat.

All this filth and clutter is waiting for you. All of it has yet to find its way into the plastic bag hanging from the doorknob on the back door.

To get to the spare bedroom, you climb the spiral staircase. The search for the spare room is short-lived. Neither of the bedrooms have doors, only doorways. Dad's room faces the street. On his wall, there's a gun rack housing Grandpa Gene's four rifles and a shotgun. The tiny three-inch-deep drawer in the bottom, where Dad keeps his spare ammunition, is left open with the skeleton key in the lock. It's been that way for so long the entire thing is covered in an eighth inch of dust. His walls are plastered with a decade of centerfolds. They mask the peeling paint and cracks in the concrete as well as the shit stains left by Sam back when his favored medium for his artistic expressions was feces farmed from his Pampers.

On the backside of those centerfolds, each woman lists their turn-ons, likes, dislikes, hobbies, hometowns, measurements, etc. It's from these lists you learn what sort of man you'll become simply by fantasizing about what sort of woman you want to one day fuck.

The spare room is little more than a storage room, a place where Dad tosses the crap he doesn't want anymore but doesn't have the time to dispose of properly. There's a bed, of course, but it's folded in half and latched into its metal frame. It's a cot, really, and all the way on the other side of the room. Before you can get to it, you have to high step through mounds of musty clothes and maneuver around piles of *Penthouses* and *Playboys* and some British magazine featuring extraordinarily hairy women. To unlatch and unfurl the cot, you'll need to muster enough strength to move two Beta players from the floor. Only then do you get a chance to take in the room around you and launch into a sneezing fit.

The sheets are damp and smell of mold. They're heavy with the humidity trapped inside the house. If you look behind the blackout curtain, you'll find the window frame covered in black spores and painted shut with Dutch Boy institutional white latex exterior. The cans still need to find their way to the dumpster. Your arm and shirt get wet from the little droplets collecting on the rubbery backside of the curtain, so you close it again and wipe your arm off with a dusty pillowcase.

The dresser is covered with spare microphones for Dad's CB radio, what's left of his CB radio, an ammo reloading press, a bag of gunpowder, a box of brass, and a cracked and dented aluminum baseball bat stained with what looks an awful lot like blood. You don't dare ask what he hit hard enough to do that to the bat. It's not the only one in the house, however. There's one within an arm's reach of the front and the back door, too. Both look as though they've seen battle.

The living room is no better off than the spare bedroom. The floor is covered with a dark brown and gold shag carpet—as are the walls, for that matter. The carpet proves oppressive, not because of the color scheme, but because of how the rug absorbs, muffles, deadens the noises of the living room. Walking in there reminds you of walking into the booth at the doctor's office when you go get your ears checked.

There are hundreds of vinyl records, hundreds more of the eight-track variety, and dozens of VHS movies—a good number of which are bootleg XXX-rated films. That last bit proves fortuitous considering you never had *the talk*. In fact, the closest you came was when you brought home a permission slip asking a parent or guardian's okay for you to watch a boys-only sexual education video, which promised to explain the changes your plumbing would soon be undergoing.

"When is it?" Grandma asks.

"Next Wednesday, at school."

"Do you want to watch it?" she says, her voice idling at a low growl, her eyes never shifting from the television screen.

You want to tell her yes, but you don't dare open your mouth. So you sheepishly nod your head. Fortunately, you're in her periphery, but unsure if you're hidden behind the frame of her glasses. If she turns to look at you and has to ask again, you get a chance to change your answer. But to be safe, you moonwalk away from her, contemplating whether it's a good time to run.

"You...filthy...pervert!" she says, snatching up the metal-handled flyswatter. The plastic flap meant for killing mosquitoes and the like falls off and flies across the dinner table. The flogging continues until you recant your earlier statement and return to school the next morning with a permission slip lacking a signature. You, along with a few other fifth-graders, spend the following Wednesday afternoon in the gym instead of watching the video and learning what an erection means and where babies come from. Instead, your first sex ed video comes from Dad's collection. *The Devil in Miss Jones* teaches you about buttfucking and blowjobs and men in diapers and girls drenched in cum and a thousand other hellish delights you'd rather forget.

You take a seat—once you move a pile of junk mail and bills to the footstool, that is. Dinner waits on a TV tray, though, admittedly, it's difficult to find your appetite. Dad's cowboy boots sit between the two chairs, and their stench overpowers the aroma wafting from the plate each time the fan oscillates. Still, as you sit, you'll notice there are places where the carpet on the walls sags, and, when the light hits just right, the strands glisten as if damp or oily. Once, when you dare put your nose close enough, you notice how it's taken on the smell he can never seem to wash away.

Each day he puts baby powder on his balls and under his pits, splashes cologne into his palm, and pats it onto either side of his neck before slicking his hair back with a dab of Brylcreem without bothering to wash his hand first.

Some mornings you get to witness this ritual, thanks to the lack of bedroom doors. The whole process only takes seconds—the same as a car wreck. You only see him standing with his back facing the door, his legs spread, his pants down to his knees, his shirttails covering his ass cheeks, and a white billowing cloud, which freshens the stale air for a fleeting moment. But you know what exactly is happening.

He calls this a Tijuana shower.

But it's time to dig in; this is your life now. A commercial comes on, so you stab your fork into the Hungry-Man and watch him peer out of his sheer curtains. They seem so out of place in his house. They look like oversized lace doilies, though they serve their purpose well enough: he can see out into his yard, but no one can see in. He loathes the thought of anyone stepping a foot into his yard to cut through the empty lot between his building and the next—so much so, he drives green metal gardening stakes into the corners of the lot and strings caution tape between them, giving it the look of an abandoned crime scene. Later, when the caution tape proves ineffectual, he replaces it with a live 110 wire. No one traipses through his yard then, save the occasional loose dog. For them, he keeps a pump-action pellet gun on the end table and aims through the tattered screen of the opened window. Their yelp is followed by a disembodied voice echoing between the two bare concrete buildings: "Get out of my goddamn yard!"

But that's not what is echoing in your ears. It's Dad's last words to you: "The day you can take me is the day you can move out."

It never stops echoing.

Echoing is the wrong way to put it, though. Echoes fade. Echoes become distant. "The day you can take me is the day you can move out" repeats the way a skipping record does. It skips until you recognize it's a gauntlet tossed at your feet rather than a way to tell you you're trapped here.

Amongst the clutter sits an unassuming leather Brunswick bag with a fourteen-pound bowling ball inside. It's the only thing in the room that isn't dusty. He hasn't bowled in a bowling alley in years. But he does take it out sometimes, and flings it into the wall he shares with the neighbors whenever they grow too rambunctious.

Dad likes the quiet. The neighbors like to entertain and argue and yell at their kids. There are times when he'll get too drunk to send it into the wall on his own, so he'll have you do it for him. Though you'll never throw it hard enough to make him happy, so you keep doing it until you are so sweaty, you can't grip it any longer.

In the drawer of that end table is a Mexican switchblade. They differ from the ones most people are used to seeing on TV. They take a bit more finesse to operate. He claims he took it off a man who groped Mom while she was pregnant. A fight ensued, and a knife was produced. He hospitalized the man sometimes and got away on self-defense when he tells this story. Other times, Dad says the guy died right there in the parking lot.

How he came to claim ownership of the knife is anyone's guess, but Mom will nod her head a single time when you ask whether it's true. That, or she is just looking at the floor, diverting her eyes away from yours, trying to avoid the subject.

A pistol lives in that same drawer, loaded and ready to go. It isn't his only pistol. He has them all over the house. Some are in plain sight. Others are tucked away. He keeps two in the living room. Another hangs from his bedroom mirror, snapped into a leather belt that looks like something out of an old Western. There's one atop his dresser. It's as monstrous as it is comical-looking, a .357 Magnum with an eighteen-inch barrel. It looks like the one The Joker, Jack Napier, wielded in the last Batman movie. A forgotten pistol sits in the closet of the spare bedroom behind a broken bifold door and beneath a garbage bag filled with his old pastel disco leisure suits.

Yet another sits on his bedside nightstand. There's no counting the number of times you wielded that one, standing over him while he slept, wondering whether you'd be tried as an adult.

PAY YOUR LAST RESPECTS

You come face to face with death well before you're ready to contemplate mortality. You're made to wear your Easter suit, which is not quite a khaki color—it's more the shade of chocolate malt. It's the last time you should ever get to wear it, since you're still a growing boy. Except Grandma Audrey wants to get her money's worth, so she'll make you wear it a little longer than you should, and she'll have to say something like "Suck it in" while she's helping you zip the pants or button up the shirt. You'll have to wear it well after you hear things like, "Where's the flood?" from those who talk in cliché and are convinced their jokes are funnier inside their head than when said aloud. Grandpa Bub, mostly.

Grandma will say, "Leave him alone, Bub."

He will say, "Buy him a new suit, Auddie."

The new suit, vest, and clip-on tie won't come until after she ushers you into a wake for the first time. It must have been somewhere in West Duluth, probably the Bell Brothers Funeral Home. Unless you're going to the cabin or to the mall to see Santa or across the bridge to the Chinese restaurant after church on Sundays, you don't remember leaving West Duluth, so Bell Brothers is a safe bet, being you can't think of another funeral parlor in Spirit Valley.

"I don't know this man" is the only thing you can think to say when Grandma walks up to the coffin, holding you out in front of her. Her hands are on your shoulders, and she pushes you up close to the casket so others can see as well—"To pay your last respects," she says, but it feels like she's using you for a walker.

This is during the early days of elementary school, so you're barely tall enough to see into the coffin, which, in your mind, means you are face to face with some dead guy.

"Be quiet, you do know him. It's Papa Harvey," Grandma whispers and gives your shoulders a squeeze—a hint to lower your voice.

Debbie is pretty upset by the whole scene, but her reasons differ. She does know this man. He lived right across the street when Grandma Audrey was married to Grandpa Gene. You learn Papa Harvey was a portly man. Was. Lying there in his coffin, his face looks like a skeleton covered in papier-mâché, caked with as much makeup as you see on game show hosts before the advent of Botox. To get you to stop asking why he looks the way he does, Grandma puts her chin on your shoulder and says his eyes are glued shut and his lips are sewn together. At full volume, you ask, "Why is he wearing makeup? Boys don't wear makeup," and you get to spend the rest of the visitation on a bench in the foyer eating sandwich halves.

It turns out the last time you visited him was at the Nopeming nursing home, out in the woods. He was still Papa Harvey then, and Papa Harvey looked a lot like Papa Noel—minus the beard. But right then, lying in his coffin, he looks like T. Charles Kingman from *Tales from the Crypt*. Maybe it's because the Nopeming nursing home started out as the Nopeming Sanatorium, and sanatoriums were meant for people with wasting diseases. Either way, Papa Harvey was allowed to waste away and die.

Grandma Audrey has no say in what you wear to the next funeral you attend, seeing as how it's her in the casket. It's the last time she manages to get the whole family together. But it is odd, as far as funerals go—seeing as how no one really cries.

A better way to explain it would be to say there were a whole lot of people sitting around in awkward silence. Auntie Harriet breaks that silence, saying, "I keep waiting for her to sit up and ask what the hell we're all staring at." A few sniffles are heard before the laughter comes.

The laughter breaks off when Grandpa Bub says, "I don't think I'll date again." He always jokes in a dry, monotone voice, but he's not joking. He's in full deadpan. There's no twinkle in either of his eyes. Neither corner of his mouth has a hint of a smile. He gets a few laughs, but no one is laughing with him. They're laughing at him.

It's the first thing he's said all day. He'd recently learned how Grandma hadn't paid their taxes in better than ten years. Aunt Bobbie made the discovery and put it together how Grandma Audrey thought Grandpa Bub would die first—due to his emphysema—and she'd move into a nursing home with what was left over from his life insurance money and pension.

At the funeral, you don't say anything. And therein lies the tragedy of Grandma's sudden stroke. You never got old enough to say what you wanted to. She gets the last word, as always.

After the processional and burial, everyone packs into Grandma's living room and dining room and kitchen. It's summer, so some are spilled outside, standing on the stoop and front yard smoking. You sit on a footstool with your back pressed up against the archway that separates the living room and dining room. And no one dares to sit in Grandma Audrey's chair at the head of the dining room table.

Over the clamoring of charming stories about Grandma's life and times, the neighbor lady, Candy—the beautician who cut your hair for free—calls attention to you. She says, "David's so quiet. He hasn't said a thing. Look," she says, "he's lost without Audrey. She was like a mother to him."

You don't respond. You cock an eyebrow, roll the back of your skull against the wall, look through the crowd toward her, listen to her yammer on about you, talking about you in third person.

You roll your head back and forth and look at the undulating chaos in Grandma's house. You can't help but think how pissed she'd be if she could see the place right then. Every room is the same when you take a lap through the house: down the hallway, through the kitchen, and into the dining room, where you whisper into Mom's ear, causing her to nod. Then you talk over the crowd, across the table, and tell Dad you're leaving, spending the weekend at your mom's house. In protest, he says something about how he wants you to be with him, but you cut him off and remind him—and Candy—how you still have a mother, and you'll be spending some time with her.

He doesn't argue. He's wounded. He pouts even. But no one is there to remind you all to not upset Richard, to not make Richard mad.

Mom'll drive you to Grandpa Bub's funeral the next summer, since you're living with her. There's a sprinkling of the grandkids there, along with some guys from the tool factory, and his surviving brother and sister. You can't remember any dialogue exchanged during the visitation. It's not that no one had anything to say, but you stood in the entryway, waiting for your dad to appear from the downpouring rain so he could pay his last respects to the man who raised both of his children.

You missed Grandpa Bub's entire funeral service because Dad missed Grandpa Bub's funeral service. This is how you learn you don't have to honor your father as the Good Book says. It's also how you learn Dad is illiterate in more ways than one.

BONES

Dad vanishes without a word on the regular. You're not alone, though. You have Jerry Lee, of course. Your best friend lives three doors down, and his mom keeps the fridge full. There are other kids too, some your age, some a little older. There's one other Indian on the block, but he's always messing with turtle shells and talking about doing bad medicine for cash. But his wife is nice enough; she feeds you, too.

Next door to him is this biker, he has a kid in your class. There's something wrong with him, and you regret saying "Hey" to him five seconds after you do so. His stepdad is this towering, lanky biker guy covered in tattoos. He keeps his hair in a ponytail, and his beard comes down to his chest. His glasses always slide down his nose, so when he looks at something far off, he looks over the tops of the frames, and it reminds you of a dragon peering at a piece of prey. Maybe there's a stronger metaphor, but, see, there's a tattoo of a dragon on his left forearm—one he put there himself. The details in the design came from him staring into a mirror while he ran the needle across his skin, so it is something of a self-portrait. To add to the image of a dragon, he lets out a huge billow of cigarette smoke when he tells you this for the first time.

And then there's his voice.

To say it booms wouldn't nearly cover it. He sounds like Charlton Heston as Moses, especially the part when he says, "Let my people go," but he talks with the rhythm and abruptness of an idling V-twin. The rest of his arms are sleeved with spider webs and fields of skulls and women with bared tits and puckered lips.

He's done a couple of tattoos for Dad. He covers up the giant initials RT and the cross Dad put on himself when he was a teenager. Now there's a tiger and a waterfall on one arm, and a giant green dragon on the other, which makes him look like some sad sort of mix of Buddha and kung fu master.

Your late-morning conversations usually begin with him asking, "Where's your dad?"

You'll shrug your shoulders and scrunch up a corner of your mouth.

He'll motion toward his front door with whatever tool is in his hand, seeing as how he's almost always tinkering with one of his bikes. When he hears the squeak of the door hinge, he'll yell out for his wife to feed you. She'll ask, "Where's your dad?" too, and shake her head with a mumbled "Fucking Richard" while she walks into the kitchen and opens the fridge.

He'll come inside and fidget with a carburetor as you take down a sandwich and some chips and a can of pop, while Zeppelin forever whispers from some speakers you can't spot.

Come to think of it, this is how you got *the talk*. It's this guy who talks to you about sex. He says, "Man, the first time I had sex, it was fun, and it felt good, and then all of a sudden it was over, and there was this giant mess. And that was it. It never got any better, man."

His wife hollers out, "Oh, shut your mouth. It's not like that at all."

He shakes his head no, hoping she won't see.

She says, "You're lucky I love you—saying shit like that."

He says, "I'm in lust with you, Mimi!"

He tells you that you got to figure out the difference between lust and love.

She yells, "You want me to leave you?"

He yells back, "I'm just trying to get him to stop thinking about sticking his dick in Ron's daughter until he learns the right way to use a condom," and looks at you over the tops of his glasses again.

He was a Thunderbird—not an Animikii, but a member of the Thunderbirds Motorcycle Club. A one-percenter. Nowadays, they fall under the Hells Angels umbrella, if you can call it that. He talks about it like it's his job. You don't know what he does other than tattoos, but he feeds a wife and three kids, and you too, from time to time. He has to be doing pretty good at his job, right? Otherwise, how could he afford the Grand Marquis?

The Triumph?

The Norton?

The Harley-Davidson?

And the Honda 100 he taught you to ride on?

You only go up and down the street on the Honda, seeing as how it's only the seventh grade and it's a street bike, not a dirt bike. Man, once you figure out how to get through all the gears and open up the throttle all the way before the street ends, there's no better feeling.

No, that's bullshit.

Once, when you're covered in oil and grease and halfway through helping him take an engine apart, some other Thunderbird comes up onto the sidewalk with his bike. The two of them talk, ignoring you, or the other guy doesn't notice you until he does. When he does, he asks, "That your boy, Bones?"

"Shit, no. I wish. He's the neighbor kid. My kid's probably off with that other retard he's always hanging around with—chasing the damn ice cream truck or whatever they do when they're not playing with each other back behind the school. Mimi tell you about that shit? They found them jacking each other off."

"I wish" is the thing that sticks with you for life.

Thirty years pass, and you'll find yourself sitting in the VA's waiting room. You'll glance outside in time to see those eyes and that beard you have inked into your flesh. The clock tells you there's enough time for you to take a stroll before the nurse calls you back, so you walk outside and up to the driver's window of a van bringing the old-timers to their appointments.

Out of respect, you wait while he finishes talking to his dispatcher with the two-way radio before you ask him, "Are you John?"

He grins. He doesn't even turn his head toward you. He sits there instead, smiling, like he's waiting for you to deliver a punch line.

So you ask, "Is your name Bones?" This makes him turn his head to look at you—really look at you, the way people do right before they say something like, "I haven't heard that name in a long time." But he doesn't say anything. He looks at you over the tops of his glasses, confused as to who you are. He doesn't say it, but the expression written on his face sure does. To answer his question unequivocally, you roll up your left sleeve and show him the dragon he put over the top of the tiny cross and initials you put on yourself when you were seventeen, and that grin of his gets even bigger.

Everything said after will stay between the two of you.

SKATER FAG

PUSHING A SHOPPING CART AROUND the supermarket while smooth jazz oozes out the speakers is hard to picture Dad doing, but he does do it, right? It couldn't have been you doing all the grocery shopping. Sure, Super America has a sprawling freezer section, and Dad sends you for odds and ends as well as movies on Friday nights.

One night, while walking home across the football field with a gallon of milk in one hand and a six-pack of two-ply in the other, you come upon a half-dozen kids ganging up on this one other kid with a side spike and a rattail.

He's clinging to his skateboard like his life depends on it, or maybe he knows what will happen if they get a hold of it. They're shoving him, calling him a skater fag. He's not even trying to fight back. It would be stupid for him to try.

He's smart.

He's trying to make it to the break in the fence. Trying to get away.

There are two sets of brothers. Both big brothers sport mullets, but it's called hockey hair here. The little brothers both have buzz cuts. They stand back and watch, echoing the last half of the last thing their big brothers say. The two other tough guys have their hair spiked as high as it'll go. They both stink of Aqua Net from clear across the football field.

They're all taking turns pushing him toward the biggest of the big brothers, the one with the biggest mouth.

None of them notice you watching from outside the glow of the streetlight until you sprint at the biggest brother with the biggest mouth and send him headfirst into the chain-link fence. Everyone watches him bounce off the fence and flop onto the turf of the football field.

Right then is when the other kid with the side spike and rattail makes a run for it.

The others scramble off into the darkness the way feral cats do when you flip open the dumpster lid back behind the house. Then it's only you and the biggest brother with the biggest mouth, who you kick and stomp. You don't punch or hit him. You can't. You didn't even bother to put the gallon of milk or six-pack of toilet paper on the ground.

A couple days later, you're sitting out on the front stoop. The kid, who clung to his skateboard, it turns out, lives three doors down, is sitting on his own stoop. After a while, the biggest brother with the biggest mouth walks by with a split lip and a black eye and his left arm in a sling. He tries to give you a look, but he's bruised so bad his sneer looks like a mix of that thing Elvis did with the corner of his mouth and someone smelling a fart.

His whole face quivers.

Once he's out of sight, the other kid looks your way and asks, "Did you do that?" and you nod your head, so he walks over to you and holds out his hand and says, "I'm Jeremy."

Jeremy is what you'd call a fixture in your life after that.

He is starting the sixth grade, you are starting the seventh. He lives with his mom, you live with your dad. He doesn't have a big brother, and you don't have a little brother, but now you each have a best friend. He teaches you to ride a skateboard, you teach him to stand up for himself. You take turns dumpster diving for last month's issues of *Guitar World* and *Guitar Player* behind the gas station, searching for tablatures which you'll hammer out over and again until your fingers become calloused and your parents grow sick of the songs you try to play.

The concrete cube of a building the two of you live in is built on the cheap, so there are some pretty cool nuances. Like, if you close the bathroom door and yell into the toilet, Jeremy can hear every word you say and every note you pluck. When it's raining, it's how you practice and do your best to one-up one another. Not that Dad would let you take his guitar out of the house, or let Jeremy touch it.

The toilet telephone is how you learn Jeremy's uncle is messing with the girl next door. She's not old enough for him. But he's old enough for prison. You don't think about calling the cops. You think about kicking his ass. You're jealous. She's making out with him while you're stuck trying to take a shit so quietly they can't hear you through the wall.

Later that day, you go looking for Jeremy at his grandma's house. Jeremy's uncle says something about you being gay with his nephew, so you slam your left shoulder into his chest and land your right fist right where his jaw meets his left ear. He drops his beer and follows it to the floor.

It's the last fag comment out of him. But he never says fag. He does this thing, this onomatopoeia, that sounds like a fart noise or a chuff, with a heavy eff sound to it. He and all of Jeremy's uncles called you the Phttt Boys. Called. Past tense.

When Jeremy starts junior high, he starts fights, and you finish them. You toy with the idea of letting him get his ass kicked until some jock stalks you through the hallway calling you a skater fag, too. That's when the light bulb comes on for you. When you square off with this jock, you don't do anything but stand your ground. He pushes you backward, calls you a bitch, and leaves you there.

There's no why for what you do next, it's just what happens when instinct has to fill in the blanks.

He turns away from you to grab a drink from the fountain before heading to class, and you lift him by the back of his shirt collar and slam his face back down, breaking the porcelain basin, leaving it hanging from the pipe. He tells the nurse the stairs leading to the football field are slick and wet from the rain. And everyone watching figured out not to call you, or anyone else, a bitch nor a skater fag as long as you were in earshot.

The spring of the ninth grade comes, and Jeremy watches the bumper of a stolen '77 Chevy Caprice Classic nail you right above the knee and send you spinning through the air before you bounce off the windshield and smash face-first into one of the concrete planters the city uses to pepper some shrubbery through downtown Duluth.

Jeremy comes with you to the emergency room, where he waits for the doctors to say you're okay. While he waits, he fingers the driver for the police, who find the guy hiding in an alleyway. Jeremy is still there the next morning when Mom is finally allowed to come to the hospital.

Mom was at home when the hospital called. She was making pancakes, making breakfast for dinner, and can't come to the hospital because the house is better than a half hour away. They might need to operate because your head is bleeding and your right leg and left arm are pretty well mangled, and they don't know what they have to do to fix you, and they'll need her permission to do anything involving cutting you open, so she has to stay by the phone.

There's a telephone in the kitchen, so she stays making pancakes, and because the house is better than a half an hour out of town, she shops at Sam's Club, so she's still making pancakes when her husband comes downstairs the next morning looking for his lunch to take to work.

He works at the hospital where you've been admitted, so he gets to see you before she does and before he heads down to the cafeteria to rip out the asbestos.

He says, "You'll do anything to get out of doing work around the house, huh?" but brings you a bag of burgers and fries from the greasy spoon diner down the street: you're hurt, not sick.

Twenty plus years later, it's you who sits in the hospital waiting room. They give you a pager—the kind most restaurants use when there's a line. Each time it erupts with flashing red lights and that unignorable trembling, you're told when the doctor opens Jeremy up, when his heart is taken offline, when his heart is beating on its own, and when he's stitched and stapled back together.

The doctor tells you he fixed seven blockages, but there was another too small to fix, and another yet that'd been clogged so long it bypassed itself. But last month, when the son of a bitch asked you to be his family advocate, Jeremy said he might need two or three stints, nothing major.

He never makes it to any of your weddings, but he asks you to be his best man. On the day of the wedding, you show up early at his fiancé's parents' house to learn a thing or two about a traditional Hmong wedding.

The first thing you learn is you won't be his best man; you'll be his chief negotiator. Not like there are any others from his side of the family. There's a lot of ceremony, translation, and drinking some shitty beer. There's an offering of tobacco to the elders and ancestors, which isn't much different from your traditions. There is a slew of questions lobbed from one side of the table to the other, including whether there are any unresolved issues between the bride's family and the groom's. Since he's a Finlander from northern Minnesota and her family comes from somewhere in Asia, it's not an issue. There's lots more drinking, a swallow after every question, making most fade from memory, except the last one: whether she is promised to anyone else. The answer is a quick one: no, she's ugly, no one else has asked after her.

With the air callously cleared, the bride price is paid to her parents—five thousand dollars, a sum decided upon by the eighteen Hmong clans, which you get a cut of for your time. Then the men gather around a table of food prepared by the women.

There's toast after toast of the same shitty beer and some clear crap that could peel paint. It has a name you couldn't pronounce if you tried, and the Hmong man sitting next to you does try, but he's been drinking as long as you have. Several times you lock eyes with Jeremy and tell him it's a great wedding, a great wedding, really, a great wedding, and then you ask: where's your wife? Meaning: why aren't they seated side by side? Why is she stuck out in the kitchen with the other women, simply serving the men on her wedding day? You're not ignorant of their culture, you're just wondering why he asked for all this.

Eventually, it's announced the wedding party must leave the parents' home, the way a bartender announces at closing time how you don't have to go home, but you can't stay there.

You'll have to make it home a hundred and fifty miles north, fueled by innumerable cans of crappy beer and who knows how many boiled chickens. On the way to the car, you make sure to tell Jeremy's new wife it was a really beautiful wedding, she should have been there.

You do make it home, and when you do, you find what's left of a pack of cigarettes—the tobacco offering—and your cut of the bride price tucked into a shirt pocket. It's only a hundred dollars, but you set it aside. At least until you decide to buy some Chinese takeout, kind of like Jeremy did.

CURSE YOU OUT, DEMON

You wake to a burst of gunfire, the crack of a carbine, the telltale call of an AK, and thrust a hand beneath the cot to snatch up your M4 and a magazine. Instead, you *Tap to Snooze* and long for a reason to rise and greet the world. Something worth rolling out of your Sealy, Serta, Simmons, or whatever the hell the salesmen talked you into buying. Whatever it is, it'll never come close to the rest you got lying on the rocks beneath the back axle of a Humvee deep inside the Green Zone or sprawled across a pallet of Pelican cases that you clipped yourself to with some carabiners on the way back from Africa.

A pair of boots, encrusted with desert sand, peek out from the closet shelf. They're discolored, coated with dust, lying atop the cardboard box entombing the pre-lit plastic tree that hasn't seen the light of day since the last time you saw your son for Christmas.

You breathe in the world around you, the putrid breath of Bentley, a North American shelter hound you brought home right after things got really bad, right after your two-room apartment got broken into. He knows the dreams are back and nuzzles you with all his ninety pounds, thinking you cannot have nightmares while you are awake. He's hungry and needs to take a lap around the block, too, so he shakes his head, and the flapping of his ears bounces off the bare walls with a clack, clack, clack sound.

You miss waking to the smell of FAN hanging in the air: feet, ass, and nuts. Not that Bentley's breath burns your nostrils any less. But you miss the aroma the detainees cannot detect coming from their clothes, their sleeping mats, their blankets, themselves. It's the reason the Kurds call them *Dirty Arabs*.

They're literal people.

The detainees spit on you, but they don't take a shit and fling it at the guards like they do in GITMO. In White Sands, they tell you the detainees will masturbate into the palms of their hands and toss it through the bars when you walk by. But they don't. Not here. Not in Iraq. This isn't like Cuba. They don't tell you this during training, though. They only tell you what they've been told. They try to prepare you for the worst. They inform you of all of the above but forget to tell you they put everyone with hepatitis into cell 3-9 until one does spit, so he can go to the SHU for some solitude, so he can sleep in a little later than usual, forgo a prayer or two or five.

Their cell chief says, "We are not animals. We are not Afghanis— we do not fling shit like apes." Yet they cough and hack and blow snot into the one washtub all forty of them use to cleanse their hands and feet before prayer. It's the same washtub they use to clean the dirt off their garden-fresh vegetables, delivered daily, courtesy of the contracted neighboring farmer.

Your stomach churns watching this.

There is one man who disgusts all others. He fasts every day, stuffs food into the lining of his sleeping mat, which you let him keep once you notice him withering away. He prays facing the wrong direction, refuses to shower amongst the others—despite them keeping their underwear on all the while. They cannot be naked in front of other men.

The other detainees say he has a jinni and will perform an exorcism, if you allow. Of course you will. Your curiosity is piqued. You're as bored as they. You're trapped in this prison, too.

Inside the cell, they lie him flat on the floor atop the red arrow the ICRC painted, pointing his head toward Mecca.

Despite his physique resembling that of an elderly Christ on the cross, several men take hold of his limbs, hold down his wrists, his ankle, his elbows, his knees. Two other men kneel, cup their hands around his ears, repeat a prayer in stereo.

The terp says this should not be watched, refuses to translate, walks off.

The imam stands with his back to the corner of the cell, facing away from Mecca. The thirty-some cellmates thunder the prayer he leads. They stand, kneel, bow their heads to the floor over and again, shaking the catwalk each time they fall to their knees, causing you to close the windows, hoping to muffle the cacophony coming from their cell.

He sobs, but the voice isn't his. Neither is the tongue. None of them know what he is saying. You don't know what they are saying, but the scene still makes your skin crawl. The hair on the back of your neck would stand if it wasn't straight-razored off before you took the watch.

Time stands still until they relent. He's let up. They pray in silence.

Every completed prayer done in this life means one less time they'll have to kneel upon the broken glass they say litters the stairway to Paradise.

He approaches the bars and pantomimes for a bottle of water. He's hungry, too. Asks in a rasp to use the WC. Through the terp, you tell him he can use it for as long as he wants.

Him and him alone.

You hand him a towel and an entire bottle of shampoo, and he winds his way through a series of steel doors into the WC. The sight of the sprinkling water makes him shed both his jumpsuit and boxers and step beneath the spray, behind the waist-high wall.

You barely make it out of the way when a cellmate tosses his clothes out the window and into the trash can. Others fold his sleeping mat in two and send it through the bars along with his blanket and pillow. New ones are sent in.

Everything going in matches everything they sent out, and no one acts the wiser. The cell chief tosses a fresh jumpsuit and pair of boxers onto the floor of the WC right where the soiled pair were shed.

Impervious, Old Man Christ towels off, dresses, and makes his way back to his mat free of the smell that once radiated from him. It's the same smell that fills the street as the homeless gather outside the soup kitchen—catty-corner from your apartment—while you walk Bentley before you head to bed. They want a meal and a roof to sleep under for the night. Most of them want to forget the same things as you. Most of them end up bivouacking in the tree line of the park a block north of the place you rent month to month.

DIESEL THERAPY

THE VILLAGE OF SULAYMANIYAH IS where the food and drink for the detainees comes from three times a day. The caterers tell you not to touch the Arab food, meaning: the food meant for the Arabs locked inside the prison. Why isn't explained or qualified.

Strange as it may seem, somehow bits of metal shavings and tiny screws find their way into the bread dough. This happens so often an additional dentist is brought in to help pull all the broken and cracked teeth.

You warn the caterers one morning, tell them you think their truck is leaking fuel. They say, "No, truck good—zore-bash-ah." And you ask if they have any extra tea.

"Tomorrow, we bring special for you. Don't drink," they say, pointing to the pots of chai you hold in each hand, "bash-knee-ah."

Those who still drink the tea shit themselves silly. Most mornings, diesel drips into the chai, until your commander speaks to the Kurdish commander about responsibilities he's been tasked with: keeping the detainees healthy and safe until they hang, for one.

While working your way house to house, searching for five escapees in the neighboring village, an old man yells, "Go," waving you all away. "We bring…to Suse."

Later you learn they were kept in the basement of an abandoned cement factory. One doesn't make it back. The four who do have to heal some before a retinal scan recognizes them. "Arab fall down mountain," the villagers say, demanding their reward money for the other four.

The night the five men broke out the window of their WC, they went unnoticed by the tower guards, made it through the fence and out into what was once Kurdistan. The prison went from a silent building, thought derelict by passersby, to a shitshow of sounding alarms and searchlights. You're woken and told to go to the cellblock to await further instructions.

The fluorescents blind you during your dash to your assigned cell block. You don't ask any questions—you run, high-stepping the whole way there, wearing what you slept in: PT shorts and a brown T-shirt.

Your rock-hard cock

Flops

Flops

Flops

From one thigh to the other, over and again, the whole way there, and it won't go away with the adrenaline flowing and blood pumping and the fear of finding five freed terrorists around the next corner while your M4 sits locked up in the armory collecting dust.

Your further instructions are to get a flashlight and put on some fucking pants.

The Peshmerga bring kebabs to celebrate the return of the escapees. The dysentery returns, too. You need three bags of saline to rehydrate and take some off-brand Loperamide appropriately encapsulated in a two-tone brown and beige gelcap to stop up the works.

The man whose job it is to keep the flies off the food takes too many bathroom breaks, and they don't wash their hands over there. They don't wipe their ass either. Instead, they punch a hole into the cap of a water bottle and squeeze, turning it into a makeshift, handheld bidet.

The next time they offer to cook, you decline.

You stop eating anything not prepackaged or frozen at the factory and defrosted and boiled at the DFAC. Most days, the food on the steam tables is lukewarm by the time your lunch break rolls around, so you grab what hasn't yellowed yet, along with a slice of the fruitcake offered at every meal year-round.

The Loperamide wears off about three days later, and you've grown tired of looking for someone to stand your post, walking a quarter mile back to the E5 berthing, removing all the gear, and rolling the dice as to whether there is a toilet available in the latrine. Instead, you grab a bottle of ice-cold mineral water the prison imports from Turkey for the detainees and head into the WC, where you pop a literal squat.

You shit where the detainees do, in other words.

Later, when they get a chance to use the WC, you learn their toilets don't flush with enough force to wash away three days' worth of MREs.

"Sergeant, you use WC?"

"Yeah."

"I think you have a medical problem. You need to see doctor. I put in Sick Call request for you, okay?"

This is the guy everyone calls the Big Show because he looks like the wrestler. He stands at least six foot four and wears his hair feathered with a close-cropped beard.

Before he was the Big Show, he was Will. Will was his codename when he worked as an interpreter for the US Army. But then he sold intelligence to the takfirs or Wahhabis or Al-Qaeda and got several soldiers killed and will one day hang for his crimes.

He helps you, though. Together you run a tight ship. No riots erupt on your watch.

One day the SERT commander is making his rounds while you conduct shower call for your cells, handing out Ziploc baggies containing toothbrushes and disposable razors. Each man has a baggie assigned to him, and each man is responsible for its return. If something goes missing, then all of them will be stripped naked and searched by a team of Americans and Kurdish Correctional Police until the item is found, even if there are six inches of snow on the catwalk and all they have to wear is their flip-flops. They learned that the hard way.

Everyone calls the SERT Commander "Tiny," even though he stands nose to nose with the Big Show and comes in at about 325 pounds with all his gear.

That day, Tiny asked the Big Show if there would be any trouble.

"No, no trouble," the Big Show said.

"I'm not worried about you giving me trouble," Tiny smiled, "but are you going to give the sergeant any trouble?"

"No, I am good for Sergeant Monday," he said, taking another baggie and handing it to the next detainee in line. "Are you wanting trouble with me?" he asked Tiny before pointing out, "You are big man. I am big man. We fight: maybe you win, maybe I win."

"What about Sergeant? Are you going to fight him?"

"No! He is no good in head," the Big Show said, widening his eyes. "He is like small dog."

See, once, while instructing a new KCP trainee how to secure a cell after a hygiene call following the midday meal, you yell to the forty men inside, and they get behind the red line.

Then the KCP nods to you, lets you know they're kneeling on the floor with their backs to the door, and it's okay for you to walk through the WC into the cell to secure the inside door while he watches from the catwalk. But when you swing the steel door open, the Big Show is standing there, puzzled. He asks, "I go behind red line?" You nod yes and step back out onto the catwalk and yell for the terp to tell the trainee again. And the terp tells the trainee step by step how this is supposed to work, again, and he nods again, and you make your way back into the cell again. But this time, one of the detainees stands to pray, and the trainee loses all sense and locks you inside the cell, slamming and latching the door which lets out to the catwalk, punctuating his fear by padlocking the sliding steel bar in place.

Hearing the sound of metal sliding against metal and the padlock clicking into itself, you move faster than can be put into words, and then scream through the barred window to be let out of the cell.

But the trainee doesn't move.

You scream to the entire prison, locking eyes with the trainee—who is too afraid to move—until someone pulls the keys from his hand and lets you out. That's when you snatch all five-feet-nothing of him by the collar and march him to his sergeant who marches him to his colonel, who makes sure he never steps foot inside Suse again.

Back inside the cell, the Big Show stands by the bars, shaking his head, talking about how stupid KCP is, and asks, "What happen I grab you?" raising his open hands to the height of your neck.

You lock eyes with him and hold out your hand and say, "I grab you."

He looks down at your hand, palm up, at the height of his ball sack, and says, "This no good. You do not touch men this way."

"If I touch you this way," you say, folding your fingers into a fist, pantomiming squishing his grapes, "you won't be a man anymore."

The Big Show makes this wobbling hand gesture like Americans do to say something is *so-so*, but for him, it means he can't believe this shit. He's done fucking with you. He respects you. He has to. He's culturally conditioned to—simply because you grew a pornstache like Saddam once grew, but he thinks you're certifiably crazy, too, because of the dragon that's crawling across your skin, and the Popeye sitting next to it, and the anchor and the pin-up girl wearing only a white hat and the myriad of sea life that signifies you're a Sailor—from the sea, as they say—*hezen-daryayi*, but they turn it into *Has he diarrhea?* and they don't get your ranks, all you petty officers. Petty means insignificant to them, so you let them call you Sergeant.

The guy in charge of the cells next door is a Navy diver, and he calls himself Sergeant Sunday when the Big Show asks his name, so the Big Show looks at you and says, "And you are Sergeant...Monday?" and you go with it for the next nine months, and he never calls you out on it since you're carrying a taser and a bottle of OC the size of a fire extinguisher.

Another time, while handing out forty roast beef sandwiches that are sealed in cellophane—something they've never seen before, but something you've seen in every single gas station grab-and-go cooler across America—the Big Show comes to the bars and runs another line of Bob's Everything Sauce across his sandwich and asks, "What is this?" pointing at the shaved, roasted meat. "Is good. Not Kurdi food."

You shake your head and tell him it's American, so he asks if it's beef by mooing, and you say, "No, it's…it's ah…" snapping your fingers and looking off toward the ceiling.

So, then he asks what it is again, bleating like a lamb this time.

Again, you say, "No."

At that, he shrugs his shoulders, laughs, and woofs like a dog, but you snap your fingers again and oink like a pig and watch all expression leave his face while all chance of him entering Paradise leaves his afterlife and he chokes on his last bite of purported pig smothered in Bob's Everything Sauce. But it's what he gets for not reading the label. So then, he gets to watch you pull an extra sandwich from the box and slather it with sauce and moo at him while you walk to the other cells.

When you look back, he's peering into the trash can where he tossed the rest of his roast beef sandwich, unblinking.

In the accompanying cell awaits a problem child who developed a habit of mocking and undermining the guards, making the smooth day less so—day after day—until there is a shift in power and the delay between the issuing of orders and the carrying out of said orders can no longer be overlooked.

He's a celebrity of sorts, famous for beheading a French journalist on Al Jazeera. Remember the video? There's a man in an orange jumpsuit kneeling, staring blankly, defeated. Standing above him is a man shrouded in black clothing, wielding a machete like the one Aladdin uses in the cartoon when he finally gets tough. Then he hacks off the guy's head. But it takes a few tries.

Now that shrouded man wears a yellow jumpsuit and is waiting for you in the WC with his nose an inch from the wall. His eyebrows damn near touch too. This is a guy you can pick out from the crowd while they pace out in the rec yard. He looks like the spokesman Geico used before the little lizard. The Kurds pulled him from the line of men while they walked back from the rec yards, and you have the youngest Kurd you can find search his person.

Random searches happen every day when the detainees return to their cells. This one is done to separate him from his cellmates, from the men who'd begun to listen to him, respect him, and who'd stopped listening to their cell chief.

He believes the Koran states all Americans must be cleansed, but you inform him the book was written about nine hundred years before America was a thing. You ask him—through the terp—to show you where it says it, but he's illiterate. He has to admit he's bullshitting his cellmates during his impromptu sermons. You've embarrassed him. And now he's been undermined, too.

Checkmate.

Having the youngest KCP officer on the cellblock search him is the greatest disrespect you can dole out from your toolbox, aside from lifting your boot off the floor to respond to any special requests the detainees make. In case you dozed off during the four-hour-long cultural sensitivity training PowerPoint, in their eyes, showing them the bottom of a boot is the same as flipping them the bird. To add insult to injury, you have the terp write *la* with a sharpie on the bottom of your boots. So, your *la*, your no, becomes a fuck no to any and all requests.

The goal isn't to upset them, it's to quiet them, and get on with the already scheduled program. There's a nearly nonstop list of checks and calls and counts and accountability measures to be completed during the twelve-hour shift. You don't have time to cater to some mass murderer's missing creature comforts.

This all takes place post–Abu Ghraib, by the way, so your job is to treat detainees with dignity and respect, not to strip them naked and stack them into a pyramid or parade them around on leashes. But their rumor mill works at a staggering speed and in comically hyperbolic degrees, so when the three of you enter the WC and instruct the Kurd to lock you in, he gets uneasy.

You stand behind the detainee, Sergeant Sunday stands on his left side, but within his peripheral vision, and that big John Coffey–looking bastard who we'll call Sergeant Smith stands to his right side, leaning against the door to the catwalk.

The three of you calmly discuss his crimes that lead to his apprehension, how his disruptions must come to an end. You put an extra husk in your voice, speaking inches from his ear the way a lover would.

He doesn't speak a word of English.

You can talk about anything. Even the food from home you miss, and you do. Bananas Foster from Landry's. Tacos from 4th Street Market.

Each time you start a new sentence, and a new wave of breath brushes his skin, he shudders.

Seeing how shaken he is, you pull on a pair of gloves and take hold of his shirt sleeves—bring his arms out to his sides, pinch his palms between your thumb and forefinger, rolling his wrists until his palms point skyward. He doesn't need to hear the command to spread his feet apart, he just does it. By then, it's expected of him. Whether he likes it or not, he's institutionalized.

Your left foot is placed alongside his right foot, and your left knee is placed behind his right knee. If he moves, twitches, you can toss him to the floor by rotating your knee to the right. If he lowers his arms, indicating in any way he's thinking of moving toward you when you're searching a leg of his jumpsuit, you can stand up with your shoulder between his legs and send him tumbling to the concrete floor. But that's only if Sunday or Smith do not flatten him before you get the chance.

First, you slap his ankle, and he lifts his foot into the air robotically. He knows the drill. The flip-flop is handed over to Smith, who inspects it—looking for anything jammed into the foam sole—while you spread his toes apart, looking for the sake of looking.

Every inch of his body is squeezed, patted, pressed on. Your hands go in his pockets. His ass crack is credit card swiped. His pecker is pulled away from his scrotum, his balls are moved to the side. Every crevice is checked twice.

Before you're done, you check the calluses on his hands, run your fingers through his hair, tilting his head back the way you do with a PEZ dispenser. His mouth opens—wide—and his tongue turns clockwise, then counter-clockwise.

Satisfied, you step away and let Sunday search him. All three of you search his person until his demeanor, his posture, is no longer one of a strident, murderous man bent on leading his cellmates into some sort of coup.

Once he's learned he is not in charge, the cell door is opened, and he's let back inside, still quaking, still crying, with the chest of his jumpsuit sprinkled with tears and the crotch soaked with piss. His cellmates look at him, and he looks at them, staring blankly, defeated. They make like the Red Sea for him and let him move back toward his sleeping mat. No one places a hand on his shoulder to console him. No one looks toward the door, toward the three of you. Some turn toward a corner of the cell to pray to Mecca once more. Some gather in groups to be led through the pages of the Koran by someone other than him. No one pays him any attention or gives him any more credence after that. He disappears and becomes another numbered detainee waiting for his sentence to end.

IF THESE WALLS COULD TALK

Fear is a funny thing.

Roosevelt proclaimed: *The only thing we have to fear is fear itself.* Whatever fear festered in him, radicalized him, soaked his jumpsuit in piss, was laid dormant after that afternoon come-to-Jesus in the WC.

Howard Phillips Lovecraft was a bit more insightful when he said: *The oldest and strongest emotion of mankind is fear, and the oldest and strongest kind of fear is fear of the unknown.* That is the fear that broke him: the fear of what would happen to him while locked in with a trinity of infidels. The fear of the foreign language tossed around the room. The fear of an enemy's breath on his skin as he stood helpless. The fear of being locked inside the walls of a prison, watching Kurdish men prepare to take the reins over him, knowing, one day, the keys will be handed off to them—after generations of Arabs gassing, murdering, robbing, raping the Kurdish people. The fear of being kept behind the same bars where some of those same Kurds were once imprisoned, but now they stand on the outside of the bars and stare inside the cells, pacing, waiting for the day the helicopters and Humvees take the Americans elsewhere.

Somewhere within the confines of the prison yards lay the bodies of over forty thousand Kurds who were tortured to death, assassinated, starved until they withered away—their husks piled into mass graves.

You remember pictures from a PowerPoint showing new construction needed to convert the place into an operational theater internment facility, and the cementing of the inner courtyard. The photos of the older construction looked patchy at best, like every scene in every horror movie where the killer hid the bodies in the basement and threw some new concrete over the top.

Another rumor speculates the bodies were buried beneath what is now the farmer's fields surrounding the FOB. The uncultivated areas were known to be full of leftover landmines from the Iran-Iraq war, while the cultivated fields were well-fertilized crops.

Once the courtyard is cemented over and turned into rec yards, the detainees spend an hour each day outside while their cells are tossed, searched, and their only possessions rifled through. In exchange, they get to breathe in the fresh mountain air. Some see green for the first time in their lives. Rumor worms its way from cell to cell until they all become convinced they're being held in Iran—home to 75 million Shiite Muslims—a crushing thought for the twelve hundred or so Sunni detainees who once entertained escaping.

They don't know they're being held in one of a dozen buildings built for barracks by the Russians to help fortify their border during the Iran-Iraq war. Most weren't alive then. Construction started in '77, so their ignorance is understandable. Especially once you consider the succession of dictators who treated their history books like an Etch A Sketch.

The mountains mystify those who take the time to look up. Others keep their eye on the ball and play soccer in the rec yard. At night, if they're good, they get to watch the DVDs brought by the International Committee of the Red Cross and Red Crescent. They have a choice: last year's FIFA World Cup tournament, or *Tom and Jerry*—the cartoon cat and mouse.

Watching them watching children's cartoons, sitting cross-legged on the floor, staring at the caged television set with undivided attention, silenced by the slapstick violence, is a sight you'll carry with you as long as dementia doesn't riddle you. The delight on their faces is childlike. The same as a child's face aglow with birthday candles while waiting for their friends and family to finish singing the song so they can stuff their faces with cake and ice cream and tear into a stack of presents meant just for them.

This is the Third World, though, and the power grid does waver.

That's not something said with a sly smile, hinting how a breaker switch could be flipped and the scene on the television would shrink to a pinhole of light and ruin their evening, all for the sake of some sadistic pleasure.

When the prison does go black, there is confusion on everyone's part. The radios crackle to life with overlapping checks to make sure they still work. There's no word from whoever is in charge; they've lost power too.

Only the battery-operated handhelds can transmit.

Inside the cell, there is a growing murmur, and an eventual, "Sergeant, Sergeant?" to which you reply, "No shit!" and turn to double-time down the darkened catwalk toward the center stairwell, where the office awaits.

You'll step into the solid blackness where you'll yell, "Flashlight!" and wait to feel the hard plastic slap the palm of your hand. But before you turn and go, you'll pause to take in the screams escaping from the opposite end of the cellblock and let go an amused laugh at the cowardice of these mass murderers and jihadists coming to light in the dark.

Turning on your heel, you make way for a shadow running the same path you did a few seconds earlier. Your eyes have adjusted some, but not as well as his. There's no jingle of handcuffs coming off him, nor do his boots clomp when he trots by you. He doesn't bother to stop for a flashlight, either, which leads you to think it's one of the KCP officers. He heads for the screams, and the cries grow louder, dominoing from one cell to the next.

Inside your cells, you can see only as far as the beam of light can pierce through the fog. There shouldn't be a fog. You've been running, yes, and huffing, but anti-fog is a punch line. Yet there's no difference when you lift the safety glasses away up from the bridge of your nose. This makes you take a literal step back and look to see if some Kurd didn't shower the cell with pepper spray to quiet their screams, but the canister hasn't moved, and the Kurds can't be seen. Not believing your eyes makes you take in a deep, forceful breath.

There's nothing out of the ordinary.

Your chest would be tight, and your nose would run with so much OC in the air. Muddled, you shine the light again and watch a swaying sea of yellow and shadow. Some are bunched in a corner; others run from one side to the other, zigzagging, dodging, and ducking. There's no making sense of the shadows, so you kill the light and squint at the petrified men inside, waiting for your eyes to adjust.

And then the mass of yellow jumpsuits moves from one wall to the corner to the far corner, toppling the piles of Korans and dumping the water from the washtub onto the floor in doing so.

Some break from the pulsing mass of yellow and cling to the bars pleading to you. Their shadow seems to taunt them the way Peter Pan's did before Wendy sewed it back on.

Horrified by your inaction, they spasm and twitch and sprint back to the mass of others. Some men fall to the floor and huddle together in a quaking pile. Convinced something extraordinary is happening—or supernatural—you feel your skin prickle, which causes you to close the window, step back against the far wall and lean into the moonlight, and fold your arms tight across your chest while you wait for the generators to wake and the courtyard lights to flicker, snap back to life with their nauseating orange glow once again, trading the screams inside the cell for the insipid needling buzz of the fluorescents overhead.

The next night, you're sitting on the edge of your rack rather than standing in front of the cells conducting an accountability check. Boredom takes a seat next to you and won't stop droning on, so you make your way to the Morale Welfare and Recreation room, where you discover it's either too late or too early to call your wife and you've watched every movie the USO sent—twice—so you haul your laptop into the detainee visitation room where you'll first open a Word document to write this all down.

Moments after the conclusion of the day's final prayer call, two guys from another cellblock enter with a single detainee, hooded and handcuffed. He'll just sit there until the next morning when his questioning will commence. But as long as he's in there, you can't be.

With nowhere else to go, you head back to your bunk following someone from the Mobile Security Unit. You're not sure who it is, but you know he's Mobile because NAVY isn't written down the side of his sweats in giant golden letters.

With the lighting as sparse as it is, the navy-blue hoodie looks black, and his silhouette reminds you of a medieval monk, one wandering around this prison searching for some solitude just like you. The two of you stroll past the female berthing, past the chief's berthing, past the first-class berthing, before he turns into the smoke pit sitting beneath the northeast turret gunner's nest.

The rain from the night before stands ankle-deep on the catwalk. The Iraqis or Russians or whoever built the place didn't exactly take pride in their work, meaning: the concrete floor is crooked, cracked, slanted, split here and there with rebar peeking through. Though, when you look for the high spots, so your shoes don't get soaked, there isn't one ripple in the puddle pooled beneath the turret gunner's nest—nor is there a soul in the smoke pit.

Back in your bunk, you slide your makeshift curtain closed, lie on top of your sleeping bag, power on your laptop once again, and type some more of this story. But your thoughts ebb back to the scene below the turret gunner's nest, and you pull your dangling foot onto the mattress.

The gunners have seen things, too.

Within every uncultivated field surrounding the FOB lies a minefield. Most accept it as fact that somewhere out there lie tens of thousands of tortured dead. The gunners have reported seeing someone out there more than once. The sighting is always confirmed by the assistant gunners, and later by the surveillance footage. When that someone fails to stop, fails to comply, comes closer, comes through the fence, comes across the fields—then the gunner must fire. At their disposal are two machine guns: the Ma Deuce and the 240, as well as the Mark 19 grenade launcher. The gunners are taught to fire to stop the threat. Not to kill. They're taught to fire a two-round burst, followed by a three-round burst, followed by another two-round burst. Anyone will tell you it's impossible to fire a belt-fed weapon and count at the same time, so you're taught to recite a poem. It's something of an abbreviated haiku:

Die

Motherfucker

Die

That someone doesn't stop when the gunner walks his rounds up to him, lifting dirt into the air all around. Sirens blare, and spotlights shine, and the SERT team suits up.

When that someone walks into the harsh light of the halogens, he falls to the ground and disappears along with the settling dust.

OUT OF THIS WORLD

"I brought you into this world, I can take you out."

That's a mantra Dad repeats to remind you how tough he is, but it's a bluff, like his welcome home speech: "The day you can take me is the day you can move out." Though neither of those begins this story.

They're just the underpinnings.

"You're stealing from me," he says, "you little thief." He pauses between each word in the latter part of this sentence, catching his breath, or collecting his thoughts that have long since left him to his own devices on this latest drunken stupor.

Little drops of spittle leave his lips and sprinkle your forehead, causing you to close your eyes, collect your thoughts, and let go of a long, slow breath.

You'll stop in your tracks and drop your book bag next to your feet. Maybe that's more in response to the aluminum baseball bat landing along your widow's peak, centered between the two caterpillars you call eyebrows, which is pretty good accuracy for how drunk he is. So is his saying you are stealing from him. You are stealing from him, admittedly, but not enough to make a bill go unpaid. You're only lifting enough from his wallet to take karate classes. Twenty bucks a month. You don't even take the belt tests. Those cost extra. You skip those weeks. Not that you're above scribbling his signature on a permission slip.

This is one of those life-altering moments. It's an out-of-body experience. You'll watch it all from the corner of the room. It's as if you're standing on a stepladder, looking over your own shoulder. If you were still standing, that is.

You do this weird Michael Jackson thing—the dance move he does when it looks like he's leaning so far over that he'll fall. But then he stands straight up, effortlessly.

It's like you're watching a movie of this, with the sound off. You can't hear a thing. But then someone rewinds it, and just like that, you're standing back up.

Dad has an umbilical hernia. To fix it, he needs surgery. But it's an elective surgery. Without the surgery, he gets a disability check.

That bulging belly button is where your first punch lands. He drops the baseball bat, almost tripping over it, and stutter-steps toward you. He raises his hands toward your face and throat. He loves to choke people nowadays; he's not much for hitting anymore.

Your hand returns to your face before he has a chance to fully process what you've done. The movement is drilled into you over and again by the sensei. It's robotic:

One

Two

Out

Back

Thumb to cheekbone.

Look over the tops of your fists.

The punch begins with a rotation of the hips.

The arm acts like a whip.

Right punch, left kick.

That left kick lands on his inseam, sending a testicle to either side of his tighty-whities and him to his knees. He charged at you, so he falls forward. You step back to let him fall flat on the floor, only he doesn't. His knees crash into the carpet, his beer belly and barrel chest smack the top of his thighs, his ass cheeks plop down atop his heels, his chin sits on his chest with a sweaty-sounding slap, and your back foot flies forward, driving your right knee right into his nose. His false teeth fall to the floor.

The rest is a bit blurry.

You exhaust yourself, and when you take a breath or catch one, you see he's out cold. His cheeks flutter like a snoring cartoon character. The fingers on your right hand fumble through Mom's work number. You don't dare take your eyes off him.

You can't remember much of the conversation, even seconds later when she says, "Say that again," and, instead, you say, "Come get me before he wakes up," stuff all the clothes you can into a trash bag, head to the bridge half a mile away.

Before you leave, you'll pull his 1955 Dove acoustic guitar out of the corner of the living room, give it a spin, look down the neck, admire the craftsmanship. Then you rest it up against his recliner and plant your foot where the neck meets the hollow body, leaving it lying there for him to find. You're no thief.

The calendar tacked to the kitchen door reads Tuesday, July 14, 1992.

But that's not really how things happened. You know that now. But it makes the most sense. It's the most logical puzzle piece. There are only so many options: flight, fight, or freeze.

When you are hit in the head with the baseball bat, you don't freeze—you become stunned, overwhelmed with excruciating pain, and you black out. Blacking out is a defense mechanism meant to protect the body from physical trauma. It's different from passing out into unconsciousness. When you're blacked out, you're still up and moving around. From an animalistic survival angle, it's not advisable to fall to the floor and lie there like some say you should do with an attacking bear, hoping it'll lose interest. Instead, the reptilian brain takes over and you fight until physical exhaustion consumes you.

The next box to check on the list is flight. You know this. It's a horror movie rule that goes ignored by everyone except those who survive to the end: get away from the monster—even if you think you've injured or killed it. So, you head to the bridge half a mile away. Except you don't. And whether you survive until the end of this story is still debatable, depending on how you define survival.

Jeremy says you stepped out onto the stoop with a black trash bag in hand and eased yourself down onto the cement step, staring out onto the street, as if you didn't notice him standing on the lawn in front of the building tossing a ball for his dog, Lady. He asks, "What's up?" knowing things don't look right. You tell him you knocked out your dad and your mom is on her way. You're going to meet her at the bridge, but you just sit there.

THE BEST PART OF WAKING UP

EACH MORNING, YOU SPIT OUT the night guard and stretch your aching jaw muscles courtesy of last night's medley of rehashed missions gone awry. You haven't broken a tooth since you were ordered to use it. Still, you stare at the reflection in the toaster, touching your tongue to one tooth after the other and feel the thin, sharpened edges and tongue the gash in your cheek, knowing if you make an appointment with the dentist to get them capped then the shrink will want to up your meds again.

Bentley sits and waits while you dish out his food. He knows not to move toward his bowl until you tell him. Then you'll measure two scoops of coffee and eight cups of water, which will be brewed by the time the two of you finish walking around the block.

He sits and waits by the door alongside your shoes and his leash. You wear either flip-flops or Roman sandals until the snow falls, so nothing can hide inside.

Bentley catapults himself toward a squirrel he sees through the window, and when your front foot lifts across the threshold, *U.S. Forces coming out* drowns out the screech of the stretching spring of the storm door, though you haven't uttered a word. It's ingrained, an inner monologue you can't shut off like music only you can hear.

Bentley makes his way down the stairs faster than you'd like, snapping the leash tight, and heads east. He shits, you bag it up, put it in the trash can. The trash can is full. The trash man comes tomorrow.

Wednesday.

Nordic Waste sounds like a metal band you'd listen to before you went outside the wire.

The coffee is scalding hot, but what's left from yesterday's pot sits in the freezer. It sounds like a life hack—coffee cubes, that is. It doesn't come close to the chocolate frappés you pound at the Green Bean while mortars are lobbed onto the flight line. You can't get to a bunker, and you stop trying to get to one after the first full day of R&R at the KRAB, so you stay inside and soak up the AC, order another.

The Third Country National contractors take pogs, but they won't accept the two-dollar bills Grandma Lynn puts inside your birthday card. They say, "No, sir,"

One, yes.

Five, yes.

Ten, yes.

Twenty, yes.

Fifty, yes.

One hundred, yes.

Two is fake. No good.

You say, "Mother fu—" before you stop and ask if anyone there wants to sell some pogs in exchange for two-dollar bills. Of course, some Lieuy does. He's still trying to be everyone's buddy.

The swill you brew now doesn't come close to the refreshment that washed over you with the Taster's Choice packed between your cheek and gum outside the wire, doing what you could to stay awake once the cordon searches became a bore, a complacency that'll kill you given enough time.

KCP officers show you pictures of their single sisters and cousins in dire need of a husband. They don't get the hint, how it's against US foreign policy to talk to the women there. They say, "Sergeant, you good man," handing the picture to you for the second time—distracting you from the task at hand in a place where blinking too many times can get you killed. So, you smile at the picture and make them think your interest is piqued. But the plan is to shut them up.

"In America," you say, "we don't take home a car unless we test drive it first," and the terp interprets and they get the metaphor and stuff the picture back into their billfold and say, "You no good—bash-knee-a."

They don't understand "No shit, Sherlock."

The calluses you built pacing the concrete catwalk of the cellblock soften while you wade ankle-deep through the waters of the north shore where you take Bentley to fetch and swim. The agates and granite stones slide back deeper into the lake with every step you take, making you anything but surefooted and reminded how you are home. The water steeps your bones in a cold that could only come from the Anishinaabewi-gichigami.

Bentley never sees an inch of the seven-mile-long beach for which your hometown is famous. Sand on your skin mixed with the scent of dead fish and the sight of women in sundresses and the sound of a roiling crowd baking in the summer sun sends you back to a market where all the men wear AKs slung across their backs. They say the situation is green. But no one can tell the Kurds from the Arabs or the Arabs from the Mexican-Americans or Puerto Ricans in the battalion, and they make everyone give away their uniforms before heading home, so you don't know who to watch. So you watch everyone.

HAPPY BUS

DESPITE RETIRING TO THE AIR-CONDITIONED city that is your hometown, you still haven't gotten used to hot coffee or warm meals. Or maybe you haven't let yourself.

All this makes dating fun.

You can eat a full meal inside of five minutes, after which you stare at the woman across from you. Other times you talk until your food grows cold. You can't stop looking over your shoulder or past hers, causing her to think you're talking at her, not to her, or with her, or how you're not even listening because you're not even looking at her.

What you wouldn't give to eat some synthetic, freeze-dried, dehydrated insult to what the rest of the developed world calls food from a plastic pouch on the back bumper of a water truck while waiting to hear "We're a go" after the chaplain wraps up his heartwarming little speech and a prayer—the same one you listen to every goddamn time you're voluntold to go out on your one day off from the cellblock. You'll help transport detainees on these Sunday drives. Some are on the Happy Bus to process out at Abu Ghraib for lack of evidence or because they've served out their sentences. Others will hang.

The Big Show says, "I have my shackles," lifting his zip-tied wrists, "and you have yours." This makes you stop, look to the hood—to where his eyes should be—and say, "I don't have shackles." But he corrects you, saying, "You have Geneva." Chuckling, he continues, "We kill soldiers, and you give us ice cream and air conditioning. Some of us never eat three times in one day before we come to Suse."

He wasn't told far enough in advance to savor his last meal.

There are two Sailors on each bus: one in the front, another in the back, plus the bus driver who is sweating profusely. It could be argued that sweating is normal, expected. Iraq is hot at this time of year, but it's a dry heat, so it's not a normal kind of sweat he's perspiring. It's more likely a nervous kind of sweating.

Because they're merely hooded and zip tied, no one is allowed a weapon—only a taser or a can of OC. It's safe to assume the driver isn't the only one who finds himself a little on the nervous side.

Some of the detainees like to pull their zip ties tighter and tighter until it cuts into their skin, causing them to bleed and turning their hands purple. They hold their hands above their head and call out, "Sergeant, Sergeant," thinking you'll take out the trauma shears and cut them free.

But you don't.

The fear instilled in you is they'll overpower you and free their friends, hence: no rifle or pistol for you. Better to have them take a taser or OC than have access to a loaded weapon. So when you hear "Sergeant, Sergeant" and see purple hands and bloody wrists, you respond with a resounding, "Too fucking bad. Wait till we get to the airfield."

At the airfield, they'll get double-locking handcuffs at gunpoint. Belly chains, too. Then they'll be padlocked to one another in neat little rows and made to sit back to back like Forrest and Bubba, except they're chained to the floor of the plane's cargo hold. It's an indelible sight, one which reminds you of the diagrams of the slave ships in your high school history books.

Back before the GWOT tribunals began, back when your unit did transport for the guys getting released from GITMO, they got returned handcuffed and hooded, shuffling in ankle restraints back to their home countries where being suspected of terrorism is viewed in a different light. While standing with them on the tarmac, turning them over and whatnot, before the cuffs came off the wrists of the first man in the conga line, their military police began to plug them in the head with their pistols, leaving them bleeding and twitching on the tarmac. Which is why zip ties are used nowadays.

The real danger is you're guarding a busload of Arabs traveling through Kurdish-controlled territory, and the Kurds hate the Arabs for reasons they cannot articulate—they simply do. The reasons, it seems, are so steeped in tradition they're woven into their DNA, and you're well aware the only thing between them and sweet, sweet revenge is you and your teeny, tiny bottle of pepper spray. This is why you'll volunteer to ride on the spare bus. There's no one other than you and the driver. You're not even technically part of the convoy. For that reason, you're allowed to carry the M4 and ninety rounds of ammunition along with your M9 service pistol and two extra mags— forty-five rounds total. For some added peace of mind, you pack two knives, one of which is carved out of the jawbone of an American alligator—both the blade and handle in one single piece. It's sold as an oversized letter opener and kept tucked into your boot when you travel abroad, and now slid into the nylon loops on the front of your body armor. The other knife is a standard-issue KA-BAR.

Your biggest fear is the bus breaking down. But it doesn't, so you have to listen to some local radio station playing something sounding like bagpipes, fingernails scraping along a never-ending chalkboard, and a yowling cat in heat, all mashed together with the screeches of a prepubescent Arab Idol contestant who is laughed off stage but somehow still got a recording contract like the She-Bang guy.

And the driver is jamming out.

Before you leave, you message your wife, "Heading out for a Sunday drive." A code she understands and is haunted by until Yahoo! Chat pings again letting her know you are safe and sound inside the wire. But that isn't exactly true. She doesn't need to know that. She doesn't need to know you are part of a defensive unit, that you take incoming small arms fire all day long and can do nothing about it because they shoot from the MSR knowing you cannot return fire and risk hitting an innocent commuter traveling alongside them or undoing the work of the Korean construction crew repaving the road between Suely and the KRAB. She doesn't need to know they like to lob mortars into the FOB or how one finds its way onto the running track, but your call sign is Marathon and you get your miles in every single day regardless—even if it means wearing a Kevlar helmet and flak jacket. It's the same for the time spent on the basketball court. Though no one is taking jump shots.

She doesn't need to know the phone conversations don't always end because the balance on the phone card runs out, but because someone martyred themselves a few hundred yards from the SPAWAR MWR phone bank, or some fucktard violated OPSEC saying *convoy* or some other shit despite the WWII posters with slogans like *Loose Lips Sink Ships* or *If You Tell Them Where You're Going, You Might Not Come Back* littering the walls.

She doesn't need to know your R&R is spent basking in the retaliation of Abu Musab al-Zarqawi's death, jumping each time a mortar leaves another crater out on the flight line, being rocked awake by three VBIEDs, sleeping through two others along with some of the spray-and-pray that follows.

You'll sleep through this stuff once you submit to the fact you don't know which direction it's coming from. You'll put a Kevlar helmet on and lie on the floor behind a pile of extra flak jackets the battalion keeps in the transient tent and hope it's coming from the other direction. But, before you close your eyes again, you tuck yourself in using your own flak jacket for a blanket, making sure the ceramic plates are situated where they'll do some good. You still hear it. But you stop reacting. Your subconscious does take note, however. *Implanting the memory*, the shrinks call it.

You'll grind your teeth down to nothing the way a tweaker does. You wake with a few cracked teeth, others chipped, and some are broken damn near down to the gum line. But it's not really your teeth that are breaking. It's the stuff the dentist shaped around what was left of your teeth after Grandma Audrey shoved you when you bumped into her on the porch steps at the cabin, the first Friday after the first grade let out.

You tripped on the stairs and fell into her, begging her question: "Are you going to start this summer by royally pissing me off?"

For nearly knocking her down, she shoves you back, knocking you down instead. Luckily, the wrought-iron railing was there to break your fall. But that's not what you're told to tell the dentist.

You tell the dentist what Grandma tells you to say, and she waits until the next Wednesday, when you finally get it right and stop stuttering your way through it, before everyone piles into the station wagon and drives back to town.

THIS LAND IS YOUR LAND

WHEN YOU'RE LITTLE, THERE'S TALK of Irishness and being cousins with the Hayes potato people. Irish, to you, means Lucky Charms and bagpipes. You only need to hear them play a single time to know their music forevermore.

It's most likely your forevermore began while watching the Macy's Thanksgiving Day Parade splayed out across the carpet in Grandma Audrey's living room.

You can't say with any certainty where you stood along Grand Avenue, but you do remember hearing them play for the first time, in person, during the Spirit Valley Memorial Day festival. It's impossible to forget that ear-piercing sound Dopplering down the street, sending a shiver across your skin.

Once you heard their song described as the missing link between noise and music.

You hear this music, the music of your people, the supposed music of your soul, leading so many somber processionals that you don't know what to think of yourself. It's not joy or pride or a compulsion to dance that fills your heart when their song rings in your ears, but the urge to back away behind Grandma and Grandpa and the wall of all the parents and stay there until the pipes are long out of earshot.

During the sixth grade, the convention center hosts a citywide Polka Fest for schoolchildren, where everyone is made to dance competitively, in rigid formation, to a boisterous blend of accordion, tuba, and clarinet. It's a square dance of sorts, but not the same as the square dancers on Hee-Haw. There's four of you, yes: two boys and two girls, but that's where the similarities end. It's a hybrid of polka and square dancing, according to an early morning internet search.

While learning the steps, both you and your dance partner have your eyes fixed on the teacher, Mr. K, as he demonstrates the dance steps he wants you to emulate. It's all you can do not to laugh while watching a hockey coach dance the polka with an imaginary partner. Polka is in his blood, but he's all alone up there because he too is too afraid to touch a girl in the sixth grade.

And that's when it happens.

Everything about this day becomes seared onto your soul, right down to the retracted basketball hoop hanging overhead while you watch Mr. K plod across the stage overlooking the school's gymnasium/cafeteria. You know it's going to happen. It's part of dancing with a girl, but she grabs your hand way before the teacher ever says to; no one is even supposed to hold hands for this one. Instead, it's one of those dances where everyone interlocks arms and swings around in a circle—changes partners—interlocks arms again with that new person, spins around with them, then it's back to where you started. But this redheaded girl is clamped onto your hand, letting you know it's too late to change partners.

You don't pull your hand away or even open your fingers to let her know it's not okay, that it's not what you want, that you don't want to hold hands, and maybe that's because it's the first time you can remember someone touching you without trying to hurt you.

So you give her hand a squeeze too.

Mr. K tells Polack jokes most of the school day when he's not yammering about hockey. Grandpa Bub tells his Ole and Lena jokes about Swedes and Norwegians and Finlanders. But when you ask Grandma, "What are we?" she replies, "What kind of goddamned dumb question is that?" blowing a cloud of cigarette smoke your way. Then she adds her favorite adage to punctuate her annoyance: "When God was handing out brains, you thought he said 'pains' and you said you didn't want none."

Through the cloud, you see her arms folded, her ankles crossed. Her top foot shakes faster and faster until you get the hint to leave the room.

You've seen pictures of her when she was a little girl. Her hair was close-cropped, a bob haircut of sorts, and formal dresses with big buttons running all the way up to her neck. She went to boarding schools; you've heard her talk about boarding schools, but they weren't in the English countryside like they are in the books you read at school. She brags about her education and shows you the swirling cursive she learned when she was a little girl. And like when she was little, you have someone pace behind you with a yardstick while you read, listening to you, waiting for you to stumble over a word. When the rhythm of the words leaving your lips slows, the creaking of the floorboards stops, and she says, "Sound it out."

If you can't, she cracks you across the knuckles. If more help is needed, she digs her fingernails into the meat of your neck, walks you to the base of the stairs, sends you to your room.

That must be where your love of literature comes from.

After the advent of the internet, everyone can research their family roots. The truth behind Dad's black hair and ever-present tan stares back at you in black and white from a single line on a ledger, dated 1891. His grandfather, your great-grandfather, is cataloged as a three-year-old

Chippewa
Catholic
Cultivator.

Considering the surname is Québécois, a vague geographic understanding is where it ends. But his name is an action verb, and Anishinaabemowin is a verb-driven language, so that's something.

You see a flyer for a wild game community feast and veterans' powwow following the fall deer hunt and know you have to go. The powwow is a spectacular celebration and proud display of an enduring culture. The emcee reminds all in attendance of this over and again in a mix of Anishinaabemowin and English, which is all but drowned out by the sound of the jingle dresses and the vibrant regalia adorning the fancy dancers. The grass dancers too. Then you notice some of them have sleigh bells bound to their ankles. It only takes one or two of them chasing after a toddler or hustling over to an elder for that sound to drown out all others, and there are dozens of them. The euphony outshines your eardrums until the emcee's microphone cuts off with a sharp squeal. It's time for the Grand Entry.

The host drum is told to make them dance.

Your shoulders drop, shudder, with each beat of the drum. Four men make the drum thunder, calling to the Creator. There's one man situated in each position on the compass: north, east, west, south, or so it seems. It makes the most sense from the little you know. They sing in cadence until it melds into one unified voice. The cacophony of their song holds your undivided attention. It's impossible to ignore. The song of the drum sinks into your chest, massaging your heart until your heartbeat matches the rhythm of their music. Your music.

It's not the elders who lead the way into the circle of hay bales for the Grand Entry but the warriors. The veterans of the United States Armed Forces carry the official flags of the four branches along with the flag of the Nah-Gah-Chi-Wa-Nong, established by the treaty of 1854. Some are elderly, of course, vets of World War II. Some wear traditional dress adorned with patches earned in combat as well as those indicate of how high they rose in the ranks. Others wear simple street clothes.

An old man will grab hold of your shoulder and say something, but his words won't rise above the sound of the drums and bells and voices ringing throughout the community center.

He pulls you back into the ranks.

He wears a red ball cap with a golden eagle, globe, and anchor.

He is called Chibenashi.

He is an old Ojibwe warrior.

He writes about Vietnam in the form of poetry and short stories.

He does it because it helps with the trauma of combat.

He sometimes calls it his brain taking a shit.

He makes you realize surviving the peace is up to you.

The two of you have a great many conversations. Sometimes it's an elder talking to a young man, and the young man listening. Sometimes it's a Marine and a Sailor-turned-Soldier shooting the shit.

Once, someone asks why you're sitting in a tent meant for the *ogichidaa*, the Fond du Lac veterans, so you explain you were born there, and you served most of your adult life, and your father is a Finlander and Indian and—and Jim cuts you off, erupting in laughter, saying "He's a Finndian!" and waves the guy asking about your Indianness away.

When you tell Jim you've begun to write, too, that you're going to school in Santa Fe to surround yourself with Native storytellers, he says, "Just make sure it's true. Everything else—the periods, the commas, the punctuation—will all fall into place."

WHAT SHE SAID

"You don't look Indian," she says. You think about asking her what an Indian is supposed to look like: Tonto from the TV, or Blackhawk from the Chicago hockey jersey? Or do you explain how Dad liked redheads, and Great-Grandpa Joe knocked up a Sámi woman because she threatened to leave the logging camp in the middle of winter—leave them without a cook—if someone didn't make her a mother. Together they made Grandpa Gene: a Finndian.

Should you bother telling her about Grandma Audrey? Irish *and* Innu Montagnais. Her family found their way here from somewhere along the border of Labrador and Newfoundland. On the way, they lived in Ontario, then Iowa, then somewhere in South Dakota. Wisconsin too. At least, it's where she went to boarding school. Maybe that's why Dad said he is a Fugawi Indian.

"You don't have a Shinnob name," she says. She's right, you don't have an Indian name. Not like one you get during ceremony, but one like the kids you went to school with: Green Sky, Light Feather, Martin, Rising Sun, Smith. But when you look at the map of where Great-Grandpa Joe came from, you see the name of a dormant volcano—translated from Anishinaabemowin into Québécois, or by a Québécois, or however that language works: Baapagishkaa.

"I don't want my daughter wasting her time learning a dead language," she says. Her daughter was fathered by a friend of yours, who was adopted out to a white family back before they passed a law to stop any more separations. It's because of white people the language is expelling a dying breath. But how do you say so without silencing her words too? Or do you say what needs to be said and stand there looking like an angry Indian who doesn't look Indian?

"You're not enrolled," she says. "I'm only half, but you're—you're less than. My babies have to be enrolled. I can't date you anymore if you're not enrolled, you understand? You need to get a hold of them in Canada and get a status card."

This makes you quiet, makes you think, and the more you think about it, the more you wonder if that'll be the measure of a true Muslim in a hundred and fifty years' time. Still, you refuse to register your dogs with the city.

"You're a bad Indian," she says. "You cut your hair. You don't live on the reservation. You went away and joined the military. They probably made you leave, made you join so they'd shave off all your hair. I saw on a television program; it's how they make you show your shame. What did you do? You're not a drunk like all the Indians at the casino. You must not know how to be an Indian. You must be a bad Indian."

You try to explain to her, but she explains to you she doesn't care to know, it's not something that'll enrich her life. You can hear her misspelling her words when she talks. But you're not a bad Indian. Simply saying that is as stupid a thing to say as telling a little girl she's not acting ladylike as if all ladies are meant to act the same way. But you are bad at being Indian. You have the blood, but not the culture. Anything you do manage to learn comes from a book or someone else's elders. Donning regalia feels like playing dress-up.

When you were in high school, you kept a tarantula next to your bed and handled it like other kids did a guinea pig. You didn't know crossing paths with a spider is one of those trickster tales that send real Indian kids running scared like they'd seen a glitch in the Matrix.

When a neighbor killed a coyote to keep his chickens alive a little longer, you took in one of the pups and named it Wile E. He bit you once hard enough to taste blood, and you backhanded him. After that, he took kibble right out of your hand. He slept right next to your bed, got between you and whoever entered the room. He stayed with you until he remembered he was a coyote and every other animal in the house was food. There's not enough time to go on about all the coyote means to the breadth of the five hundred or so Native nations without slipping immediately into cliché or echoing a million other tellings of the coyote trickster tales. The only thing you knew at the time was how Jose Chavez y Chavez called Billy the Kid the Oblero in *Young Guns II* and he was supposed to be Mexican and Indian. Weird how he didn't consider his Mexican-ness an Indian-ness.

But your ignorance doesn't end with your adolescence.

It bothers you beyond words when you see a crow bounce off a windshield and struggle to get itself to the shoulder of the highway before being run over by another motorist. It's winter, so you know if it lies there on the concrete, it'll freeze to death before the night is through. There's no reason for its suffering when there's a wildlife rehabilitation center about a mile away as the crow flies. When you try to get hold of it, it flaps its wings and swims across the freshly fallen snow, except it can't stand up. The receptionist says it'll make a full recovery, it has fluid on its spine and needs some antibiotics and anti-inflammatories, so you swipe your bank card, and for your donation they give you a bumper sticker.

When you sit and mull this all over with a Lakota poet who brings plenty to the table of conversation, he comes to the conclusion it might be it's your father who is the trickster.

Dad talked about how he wasn't a complete failure as a father, how he could serve as an example of what not to be, and how not to act, and, because of this, you became and accomplished everything you did. Not because of your own hard work, but because he showed you what you didn't want to be. This is how alcoholics operate: able to justify anything and take credit for imagined undertakings.

So, when she says, "You don't look Indian," what you hear is, "You don't look like your father," and you have to stop "Thank God" from exploding past your lips.

He wasn't a bad-looking dude. He got married three times. Each time, his wife was nineteen years old—too young and immature and stuck around too short of a time to figure out what was really wrong with him. He wasn't a bad Indian, either. He was a bad man who happened to have some Indian blood.

If you looked like Dad—like an Indian—you'd have to look into his eyes every time you look into the mirror. You'd see him every time you brushed your teeth or plucked a nose hair. Still, trying to tell this story is like when someone asks why a marriage didn't work. The explanation falls short, and the person asking the question fails to realize the stuff they're hearing is only the parts of the story the narrator is willing to breathe life back into. You know if you tell them everything, they'll go numb, like you. Then the stories don't quite sting as much and you'll scribble down a splattering of what has popped into your mind.

But this is not a tell-all.

Some credence has to be given to how, when the story begins to show him as a shiftless old drunk who can be knocked out by a fourteen-year-old kid, they'll question who it is they should really feel sorry for, who the real monster was. You also have to consider what does it make you, beating some brain-damaged drunk and running away without making sure he's okay? Was Dad a trickster trying to teach you something about yourself, or was he a wiindigoo?

NOTE TO SELF

Two days after you finish putting the first draft of this down on paper, Dad is diagnosed with cancer, again. It's terminal this time. Past the point of no return. He's not going to get any better. He'll only get worse and one day die. The doctors won't treat his ailments any longer. They'll only set him up on a mix of sedatives and medications meant to ease his pain until he can no longer register the reality of his own body rotting from the inside out. They won't say what kind of cancer. Turns out it's colon cancer that made its way up to his brain and into everything in between. The bones too. They won't say how long he has, only that it is now in God's hands.

He missed a follow-up appointment after his last cancer treatment—right around three years ago. But the doctors said he was done. Cured. That's what Dad told Debbie. He decided against wasting anyone else's time or money after that. Yet one morning, when he tried to sit up, he couldn't. His back wouldn't bend. The bones were mush. The muscles too.

This is all secondhand information, mind you.

He does die, but it takes you another half-dozen drafts to say what you need to say.

With his last breath, the last bit of angst drips out of your pen. He's gone. Ashes to ashes. Cremated with the remains of his checking account.

Before your next birthday, the doctor shoves a camera up your ass to look for what killed your dad. There'll be no escaping being your father's son until your dying day.

Full physicals suddenly become even more so. The EKG says bradycardia. It is normally a good thing for someone who runs or bikes or works out in any way, shape, or form, but it's bad because you sit on your ass all day typing this out. There's an arrhythmia, too, and the nurse says it is so bad they can't give you some shot they were supposed to because it could send you into cardiac arrest.

Someone once said that writing this book might save your life.

It turns out it might kill you, too.

ACKNOWLEDGMENTS

THE FIRST THING I I have to acknowledge is that this collection is the severely abridged, Cliffs Notes version of events, or as my big sister said, "Bubba, you are barely scratching the surface of what they did to you."

Excerpts from *As You Were* appeared in *Mystery Tribune; RED INK: International Journal of Indigenous Literature, Arts, & Humanities; The Dead Mule School of Southern Literature; Yellow Medicine Review; Open: Journal of Arts & Letters; Watershed Review; FIVE:2:ONE Magazine;* and *BULL: Men's Magazine.* I want to thank each of the readers and editors for letting it be so.

I am eternally grateful for the guidance I received from Stephen Graham Jones while writing *As You Were.* I hope the lessons learned echo throughout whatever I commit to paper in the future.

I'd especially like to thank Michelle Dotter for pulling this manuscript from the slush pile and polishing it into what it is today.

I owe my sister, Debbie, an enormous amount of gratitude for helping me slog through memories that she tried so hard to forget for so many years.

And my father, for without you, this book would not exist. I might have even become a well-adjusted member of society. But what fun would that be?

ABOUT THE AUTHOR

DAVID TROMBLAY served in the US Armed Forces for over a decade before attending the Institute of American Indian Arts for his MFA in Creative Writing. His essays and short stories have appeared in *Pank Magazine; Michigan Quarterly Review; RED INK: International Journal of Indigenous Literature, Arts, & Humanities; The Dead Mule School of Southern Literature; Yellow Medicine Review; Open: Journal of Arts & Letters; Watershed Review; FIVE:2:ONE Magazine*; and *BULL: Men's Magazine*. He lives in Oklahoma with his dogs, Bentley and Hank.